THE IMPORTANCE OF

Bruce Lee

THE IMPORTANCE OF

Bruce Lee

These and other titles are included in The Importance Of biography series:

Maya Angelou
Louis Armstrong
James Baldwin
Lucille Ball
The Beatles
Alexander Graham Bell
Napoleon Bonaparte
Julius Caesar
Rachel Carson
Charlie Chaplin
Charlemagne
Winston Churchill
Christopher Columbus
Leonardo da Vinci
James Dean
Charles Dickens
Walt Disney
Dr. Seuss
F. Scott Fitzgerald
Anne Frank
Benjamin Franklin
Mohandas Gandhi
John Glenn
Jane Goodall

Martha Graham
Lorraine Hansberry
Ernest Hemingway
Adolf Hitler
Thomas Jefferson
John F. Kennedy
Martin Luther King Jr.
Bruce Lee
John Lennon
Douglas MacArthur
Margaret Mead
Golda Meir
Mother Teresa
John Muir
Richard M. Nixon
Pablo Picasso
Edgar Allan Poe
Queen Elizabeth I
Jonas Salk
Margaret Sanger
William Shakespeare
Frank Sinatra
Tecumseh
Simon Wiesenthal

THE IMPORTANCE OF

Bruce Lee

by Andy Koopmans

LUCENT BOOKS
SAN DIEGO, CALIFORNIA

THOMSON
™
GALE

Detroit • New York • San Diego • San Francisco
Boston • New Haven, Conn. • Waterville, Maine
London • Munich

Library of Congress Cataloging-in-Publication Data

Koopmans, Andy.
   Bruce Lee / by Andy Koopmans.
      p. cm. — (The Importance of)
Includes bibliographical references and index.
Summary: Explores the life of Bruce Lee, whose drive for
perfection led him to great success as a martial artist, teacher of
kung fu, actor, and filmmaker, despite his early death and
Hollywood's prejudice against Asians and Asian Americans.
   ISBN 1-59018-081-X (alk. paper)
   1. Lee, Bruce, 1940–1973—Juvenile literature. 2. Actors—
United States—Biography—Juvenile literature. 3. Martial
artists—United States—Biography—Juvenile literature. [1. Lee,
Bruce, 1940–1973. 2. Actors and actresses. 3. Martial artists.]
I. Title. II. Series.
   PN2287 .L2897 K66 2003
   791.43'028'092—dc21

2001007308

Copyright 2002 by Lucent Books,
an imprint of The Gale Group
10911 Technology Place, San Diego, California 92127

Printed in the U.S.A.

Contents

Foreword   9
Important Dates in the Life of
  Bruce Lee   10

INTRODUCTION
A Brief, Passionate Life   12

CHAPTER 1
Enter the Dragon   14

CHAPTER 2
The Seattle Years   29

CHAPTER 3
Discovered!   43

CHAPTER 4
Hollywood   58

CHAPTER 5
Breaking Through   71

CHAPTER 6
King of Hong Kong   84

CHAPTER 7
Death by Misadventure   100

Notes   113
For Further Reading   115
Works Consulted   117
Index   121
Picture Credits   127
About the Author   128

Foreword

THE IMPORTANCE OF biography series deals with individuals who have made a unique contribution to history. The editors of the series have deliberately chosen to cast a wide net and include people from all fields of endeavor. Individuals from politics, music, art, literature, philosophy, science, sports, and religion are all represented. In addition, the editors did not restrict the series to individuals whose accomplishments have helped change the course of history. Of necessity, this criterion would have eliminated many whose contribution was great, though limited. Charles Darwin, for example, was responsible for radically altering the scientific view of the natural history of the world. His achievements continue to impact the study of science today. Others, such as Chief Joseph of the Nez Percé, played a pivotal role in the history of their own people. While Joseph's influence does not extend much beyond the Nez Percé, his nonviolent resistance to white expansion and his continuing role in protecting his tribe and his homeland remain an inspiration to all.

These biographies are more than factual chronicles. Each volume attempts to emphasize an individual's contributions both in his or her own time and for posterity. For example, the voyages of Christopher Columbus opened the way to European colonization of the New World. Unquestionably, his encounter with the New World brought monumental changes to both Europe and the Americas in his day. Today, however, the broader impact of Columbus's voyages is being critically scrutinized. *Christopher Columbus*, as well as every biography in The Importance Of series, includes and evaluates the most recent scholarship available on each subject.

Each author includes a wide variety of primary and secondary source quotations to document and substantiate his or her work. All quotes are footnoted to show readers exactly how and where biographers derive their information, as well as provide stepping stones to further research. These quotations enliven the text by giving readers eyewitness views of the life and times of each individual covered in The Importance Of series.

Finally, each volume is enhanced by photographs, bibliographies, chronologies, and comprehensive indexes. For both the casual reader and the student engaged in research, The Importance Of biographies will be a fascinating adventure into the lives of people who have helped shape humanity's past and present, and who will continue to shape its future.

Important Dates in the Life of Bruce Lee

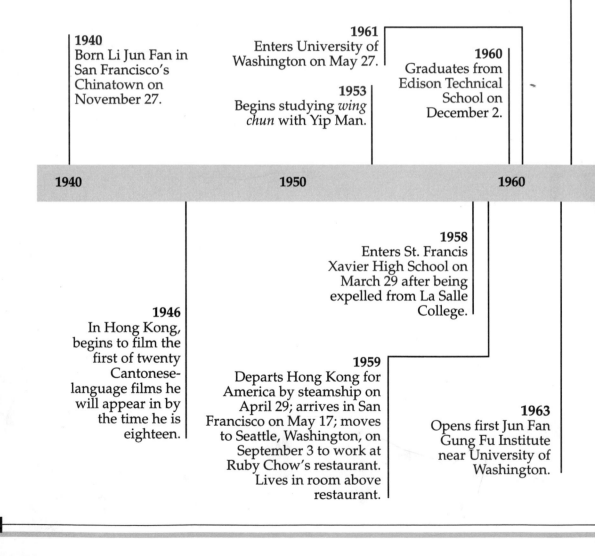

1964
Opens second Jun Fan Gung Fu Institute with James Lee in Oakland, California; performs at the International Karate Tournament in Long Beach, California; marries Linda Emery in Seattle on August 17; couple leaves for Oakland the next day.

1940
Born Li Jun Fan in San Francisco's Chinatown on November 27.

1961
Enters University of Washington on May 27.

1953
Begins studying *wing chun* with Yip Man.

1960
Graduates from Edison Technical School on December 2.

1940   1950   1960

1958
Enters St. Francis Xavier High School on March 29 after being expelled from La Salle College.

1946
In Hong Kong, begins to film the first of twenty Cantonese-language films he will appear in by the time he is eighteen.

1959
Departs Hong Kong for America by steamship on April 29; arrives in San Francisco on May 17; moves to Seattle, Washington, on September 3 to work at Ruby Chow's restaurant. Lives in room above restaurant.

1963
Opens first Jun Fan Gung Fu Institute near University of Washington.

1966
Begins work
on *The Green
Hornet*.

1967
Opens third
Jun Fan Gung
Fu Institute in
Los Angeles.

1969
Daughter Shannon
Lee born in Santa
Monica, California,
on April 19.

1971
Travels to India with James
Coburn and Stirling Silliphant
to scout locations for *The Silent
Flute;* goes to Thailand to film
The Big Boss (Fists of Fury) for
Golden Harvest Studios.

1972
In Hong Kong, films *Fist of Fury
(The Chinese Connection)* for Golden
Harvest Studios; forms Hong Kong
production company Concord with
Raymond Chow and makes
directorial debut in *The Way of the
Dragon (Return of the Dragon);* begins
filming *The Game of Death*.

1965   **1970**   **1975**

1968
Appears in *Marlowe,*
his first American
feature film, as
villain Winslow
Wong.

1965
Son Brandon Bruce Lee born in
Oakland, California, on February
1; takes screen test at Twentieth-
Century Fox Studios for proposed
series *Number One Son* on
February 4; father Li Hoi Chuen
dies on February 8; Bruce Lee flies
to Hong Kong for funeral.

1973
Interrupts filming *The
Game of Death* to make
Enter the Dragon for
Warner Brothers Studios;
dies in Hong Kong on July
20; laid to rest in Lake
View Cemetery in Seattle,
Washington, on July 31.

A Brief, Passionate Life

Bruce Lee became a legend even before his death. During his film career, he became a national hero to many in Hong Kong, and with the success of the last film completed during his life, *Enter the Dragon*, Lee became

Bruce Lee fights members of a Japanese boxing club in the film The Chinese Connection.

the highest paid actor in the world. When he died suddenly in 1973 at the height of his fame, he became a cultural icon.

Almost thirty years after his death, Lee is still a household name. His influence and example in the martial arts world is so important that a thorough discussion of martial arts in America must include a mention of him. And, although he completed only four martial arts movies as an adult, to many people the end of his career signaled death of the true martial arts film.

THE REAL BRUCE LEE

The legendary Bruce Lee often overshadows or obscures the real man. Lee was a devoted husband and father, a respected and renowned teacher, a loyal friend, and a complex man, driven toward perfection. He was not born rich, famous, or even strong. The successes of his martial arts and acting careers were due to his independence, persistence, and work ethic, as well as to his dynamic personality and energy.

As a martial artist, Lee stood apart from his contemporaries by breaking with Chinese tradition and introducing and popularizing kung fu in the West. Additionally, his independence led him to divert from classi-

Lee demonstrates jeet kune do, *a martial arts style he developed.*

cal forms of kung fu to develop *jeet kune do,* his own martial arts philosophy that is still widely studied and practiced today.

As an actor and filmmaker, Lee was a pioneer, both in the East and West. His determination to create better-quality films and to raise the salary level of his own performances revolutionized how movies were made in Hong Kong. In Hollywood, his persistent attempts and eventual success in breaking through the barrier of racial prejudice opened up opportunities in the United States for a long line of Asian and Asian American actors and martial artists.

Following his death, many biographers delved into Lee's life, trying to discover what drove him so tirelessly toward his ambitions and made him so apparently sure of his destiny. While many questions about Lee's life are disputed or unanswered, the story of what is known about him begins in San Francisco's Chinatown.

1 Enter the Dragon

Although he would spend the formative years of his life in Hong Kong, Bruce Lee began his life in America. In October of 1940, Li (Lee) Hoi Chuen, an actor with Hong Kong's Cantonese opera, traveled to San Francisco with his wife Grace while the opera was on a tour of the United States. While there, Grace discovered that she was pregnant. No one has ever said for sure whether or not Hoi Chuen and Grace planned the pregnancy so that their child would be born in the United States, but the timing was important. President Franklin Roosevelt had just signed the Immigration Act of 1940 into law. This law made it possible for the child of foreign parents to receive American citizenship if the child was born in America.

PARENTS

Hoi Chuen and Grace met in Hong Kong several years before, when Grace was nineteen. Grace's father was a great lover of the Cantonese opera and often took Grace to it. There, Grace developed a crush on the star, Hoi Chuen. She attended the opera again and again and sat near the orchestra, where she knew Hoi Chuen could see her. Ultimately, her efforts paid off. Hoi Chuen took notice of Grace because of her persistence, and the couple soon married.

Hoi Chuen and Grace, like many traditional Chinese, were quite superstitious; superstitions, especially those dealing with birth and death, are commonplace, even in modern-day China. In Hong Kong, their first son died shortly after birth. Besides being a tragedy, they thought the death was a bad omen. The Lees believed evil spirits had stolen their son and that the spirits would return to harm future male offspring. Thinking the spirits could be persuaded to leave them alone if they had a girl, they adopted a daughter, Phoebe. Their next natural child, a boy whom they named Peter, survived.

In America in 1940, Hoi Chuen left Grace with friends in San Francisco while the opera tour moved on to New York, so he was not there in the early morning of November 27, when Grace gave birth to a boy at Chinatown's Jackson Street Hospital. According to Chinese astrology, the child's birth was auspiciously timed because it fell in the year and hour of the day represented in the Chinese zodiac by the dragon, the most revered and powerful creature in Chinese legend. Grace named the boy Jun Fan, which means "Return Again," because she believed that he would someday return to his place of birth.

It is common in the United States for children of foreign parents to receive an anglicized name along with their birth name. Since Grace did not speak English well enough to choose one, a nurse at the hospital gave the boy the American name he would use later in his life in the United States: Bruce Lee.

INTERESTING TIMES

There is a Chinese curse that goes, "May you live during interesting times." Born at the height of World War II, just prior to the Japanese invasion of Hong Kong, Bruce Lee did indeed live in very interesting times. Hong Kong, located on the southeastern coast of China, became a British colony in 1842, and soon afterward the British opened Hong Kong as an imperial port. The port brought trade and a demand for labor, which meant more jobs and better wages for those living in Hong Kong than in other parts of China. Many Chinese followed the promise of economic improvement and personal freedom into Hong Kong. Among these immigrants were Li Hoi Chuen's and Grace Lee's families.

Bruce Lee was born in San Francisco's Chinatown (pictured) in 1940.

Over the next century, immigration and Hong Kong's economy increased, but so did the tensions between the British colonists and the Hong Kong Chinese. Grinding poverty lived alongside immense wealth, and overcrowding, unemployment, natural disasters, plague, and several unsuccessful Chinese uprisings against the British marred the colony's history.

Then, in December 1941, as Japan attacked the United States at Pearl Harbor, Japanese ships sailed into Hong Kong Har-bor and defeated the British navy. The Japanese occupied Hong Kong until 1945, when the Allies defeated them and the British reclaimed the island.

The cruel and oppressive rule of the Japanese during this period infuriated the Hong Kong Chinese. Japanese soldiers committed atrocities on the Hong Kong Chinese such as rape, assault, and even murder. Bruce Lee's family suffered through this period of oppression along with their fellow Chinese, and legend says that Lee used to stand on the balcony of his family's apart-

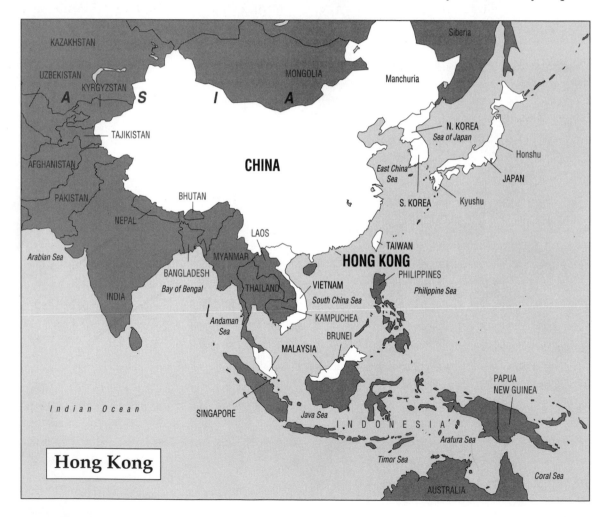

Hong Kong

British prisoners of war travel to a World War II Japanese prison camp. From 1941–1945, the Japanese occupied Lee's hometown of Hong Kong.

ment as a toddler and shake his fist in anger at the Japanese planes flying overhead.

A BUSTLING HOUSEHOLD

In early 1941, just before the Japanese invasion, the Lee family returned home from the United States to their home in the Kowloon District of Hong Kong. Their apartment was on Nathan Road, a long, densely crowded boulevard that contained about a quarter of a million people per square mile. The family lived in a small place on the second floor of an old building above some shops, facing the street.

Hoi Chuen was a landlord. He owned several apartments around the district, so the Lee family was better off than many other Hong Kong Chinese were, but they were by no means wealthy. The Lees and their five children—Phoebe, Peter, Bruce, Robert, and Agnes—lived in the Kowloon apartment with Hoi Chuen's widowed sister-in-law

and her five children. Hoi Chuen's brother had died and, as was Chinese custom, the widow and her children were taken into a family member's household. In addition, there were one or two in-house servants, depending on the need, and Wu Ngan, an orphan boy the Lee family had taken in as part of the family. Biographer Tom Bleecker describes the living conditions in the apartment:

> The Li [Lee] family lived like the vast majority of Chinese residing in Hong Kong in the spring of 1941, packed like sardines into dilapidated apartment dwellings and surrounded by an urban beehive of garish neon signs and clamourous shopfronts.[1]

There were sometimes as many as twenty people—along with assorted dogs, birds, and fish—crammed into the two-bedroom apartment, with many people living, eating, and sleeping in each room. The apartment was constantly bustling and lines for the

Lee grew up in Hong Kong's crowded and dangerous Kowloon District (pictured).

single bathroom were common. Baths were sometimes impossible because the tub was frequently used during drought conditions to hold water for cooking or flushing the toilet.

"NEVER SITS STILL"

Bruce Lee was a sickly child early on. The humidity of Hong Kong was hard on him and he was skinny, but as he grew, he developed a natural charisma and a love of physical activity. Hoi Chuen often took his son along with him to work, to the opera, or to film sets when he was working on movies. In these settings Lee developed a love for performance.

At home, Lee was full of frenetic energy and practical jokes. The family nicknamed him Mo Si Tung, which means "Never Sits Still," because he was constantly running, jumping, or talking. In fact, the only time he was not moving was when he was reading, which he did to the point of becoming near-sighted and requiring glasses from the age of six. For the rest of his life, he would always wear thick glasses or contact lenses.

Despite his love of reading, Lee did not like school. He cut class frequently, spending much of his early life roaming the streets of Hong Kong, looking for ways to amuse himself. Hoi Chuen, like many Chinese fathers, was a distant figure and not often at home. Grace could not keep track of Lee and take care of her other children and the household as well, so Lee was often unsupervised by adults. Frustrated by the repeated calls from the school telling her that her son had missed school, Grace finally told him that if he cut school he at least had to let her know where he was playing so that she would not worry. Lee did this, but he still managed to get into trouble frequently.

Lee was not worried about school, though. He was confident, almost cocky, and felt that he was special—that he was meant for great things. Grace said,

> Bruce never changed his character. He repeated the same mistakes time after time. I was disappointed with him again and again. Once I asked how he expected to earn his living if he kept on like that. He said, "I'll become a famous film star one day." I scolded him and told him that the life of a famous film star was not so comfortable as he imagined and that their lives were abnormal. I told Bruce, "You can't even behave like a normal person. How do you expect to become a film star?"[2]

LEE LITTLE DRAGON

In fact, the young Bruce Lee already was a film actor, though not a star. In 1946, when Lee was six, Hoi Chuen arranged for him to begin a career as a child actor. Lee appeared in twenty Cantonese-language films by the time he was eighteen years old.

As a youngster, Lee frequently played the roles of street urchins and precocious kids, but as he grew into adolescence, he began playing brooding juvenile rebels. His most famous role was in *The Orphan,* a film made when he was eighteen. In it, he played a street-fighting delinquent, a role that ended up striking very close to home.

TROUBLED ADOLESCENCE

Bruce Lee started getting into trouble when he began school at Hong Kong's La Salle College in 1952. Lee was hyperactive, disruptive, and unable to tolerate the rules of the classroom. He was not a successful student and grew angry and rebellious. Linda Lee, who married Bruce Lee in 1964, writes:

> Classes [at La Salle] are taught in English, even though most of the boys are Chinese and have no English-speaking background, which was Bruce's case. Scholastically speaking, Bruce's grades at La Salle were average at best. I believe that his frustrations at that point in his life were mounting, and as a result he repeatedly found himself in trouble at school. . . . [H]e did what many adolescent boys struggling for their identity do in troubled times—he turned to the streets and his peer group.[3]

THE TIGERS

At La Salle, Bruce Lee became the leader of a small gang called the Tigers. The gang sought out British boys to fight after school. The Chinese hated the British almost as much as they hated the Japanese. After the Japanese occupation, Hong Kong had returned to British rule. Even though life under the British was better than under the Japanese—the Japanese openly brutalized the Chinese people while the British usually oppressed the Chinese in more subtle

A Pugnacious Childhood

Much of Bruce Lee's childhood was spent fighting in the streets of Hong Kong. In a 1972 autobiographical article for a Taiwan newspaper, reprinted in Bruce Lee: Words of the Dragon, *edited by John Little, Bruce Lee remarks on the violent nature of his childhood.*

From boyhood to adolescence, I presented myself as a trouble-maker and was greatly disapproved of by my elders. I was extremely mischievous, aggressive, hot-tempered and fierce. Not only my "opponents" of more or less my age stayed out of my way, but even the adults sometimes gave in to my temper. I never knew what it was that made me so pugnacious [combative]. The first thought that came into my mind whenever I met somebody I disliked was: "Challenge him!" Challenge him with what? The only concrete thing that I could think of were my fists. I thought that victory meant beating down others, but I failed to realize that victory gained by way of force was not real victory. When I enrolled at the University of Washington and was enlightened by philosophy, I regretted all my previous immature assumptions.

Lee was a hot-tempered child who got into many fights.

Reclaiming Hong Kong, British forces round up Japanese troops after four years of occupation. Lee, like his fellow Chinese, disliked the British presence almost as much as the Japanese.

ways—the Chinese felt a deep resentment against the British colonizers.

Lee's gang often instigated and frequently lost fights against the larger British boys; however, Lee would never admit to being beaten. Even so, as a teenager in Hong Kong, Lee usually returned home beaten and bruised, to the displeasure of his parents. Hoi Chuen and Grace did not approve of his fighting. When Hoi Chuen was around, he punished Lee, sometimes by hitting him or by placing many restrictions on the boy's activities. Grace, on the other hand, had a soft spot for her son even though she did not like his fighting. She often protected Lee from Hoi Chuen's punishment by not telling her husband about the fights.

KUNG FU AND YIP MAN

In China, children take up the martial art of kung fu as commonly as kids in the West take up sports such as baseball. At thirteen, Lee was the leader of his small gang the Tigers, but, as William Cheung, a childhood friend of Lee's, said, "The Tigers were just eight people who got together, but they weren't all that tough—they got their fur singed a lot."[4]

Lee's gang got beaten frequently enough that he became frustrated and demanded that his parents enroll him in martial arts classes. Grace agreed, convincing Hoi Chuen that it was for the best that their son be able to protect himself, and they gave him money for lessons. Lee persuaded his friend William Cheung to introduce him to Yip Man, grand master of a kung fu system called *wing chun*. Bruce met with Yip Man in 1954 and, because of Lee's minor celebrity as a film actor, Yip Man accepted him as a student on the spot, which was unusual.

WING CHUN

The history of *wing chun* mingles with legend. In about 1720, troops of the Chinese Manchu dynasty invaded the Shaolin monastery where kung fu had originated in the sixth century. The troops were to destroy the temple and kill the Buddhist monks who lived there. The monastery was renowned for its hand-to-hand combat, and the Manchu government wanted to eliminate any chance that the monks would threaten the new dynasty. Most of the monks were killed in the invasion, but a few escaped. Among the escapees was Ng Mui, an abbess and the only female member of the temple to escape. She went into hiding and used her secluded time to study nature and how it related to kung fu. Based on her observations, she developed a new style of kung fu that, in part, mimics the movements of animals.

Meanwhile, another survivor of the Shaolin temple settled in a village and fathered a child. The child grew to be a beautiful girl who attracted the attention of a tough local gangster. The gangster pursued the girl and demanded that she become his wife. Although the girl did not want to marry him, she had no alternative—she could not run away because she could not support herself on her own.

Fortunately, Ng Mui heard of the girl's situation and secretly took her away into the wilderness. For three years the girl studied the kung fu style Ng Mui had developed. When the girl returned to the village, the gangster accosted her in the village square. The girl said that she was ready to marry but she could only marry a man whom she could not defeat in hand-to-hand combat. The gangster agreed to fight her. To everyone's surprise, the girl won, and the gangster left the village in disgrace.

The girl's name was Wing Chun, and the style that she learned from Ng Mui took her name. Wing Chun passed her training down, and six generations later Yip Man learned the style. Yip Man mastered *wing chun* before beginning to teach at age fifty-eight; he was in his sixties when Bruce Lee, who would become his most famous student, began studying with him.

"FIGHTING CRAZY"

What Lee liked about *wing chun* was that it was designed to defeat an opponent by using as little effort as possible and involved the least amount of risk of being hit. Because he was small and could not afford to be hit, especially by larger opponents, the latter point was particularly important to him. Lee took to the style with an obsession. He was always practicing, kicking trees, hitting his knuckles on a stool during dinner to toughen them, and picking fights with anyone he could find.

Lee became a bit of a bully during his teen years, particularly as his martial arts

A WAY WITH THE GIRLS

Bruce Lee's reputation and style made him popular with girls his age. In her book The Bruce Lee Story, *Linda Lee describes Bruce's early dating years in Hong Kong.*

By the time he was 15, Bruce was a considerable figure among the kids living in his neighborhood of Kowloon. He was very good-looking and began to take an interest in girls. His brother Peter recalls that Bruce would spend up to 15 minutes in front of the mirror, getting his hair just right, making sure his tie was properly adjusted—a born perfectionist. His looks, self-confidence, and reputation as a battler, meant that he had little difficulty attracting feminine attention. His attitude toward girls was nicely balanced too—just the right mixture of self-assurance, sensitivity, and easy grace. In short, he brought a formidable array of charms to bear on females who came within his orbit. He even proved to be quite an expert dancer, winning the Crown Colony Cha-Cha Championship in 1958. He kept a list of 108 different steps on a card in his wallet. Whatever Bruce decided to do, whether it was fighting, acting, dancing, or being a friend, he always gave it his all.

---

prowess increased. He bullied classmates into doing his homework for him (something he would regret later in life when he was struggling to catch up in his education) and he set out to get into fights as often as possible. Robert Clouse writes:

As soon as he was old enough to challenge another boy on the street, he did so. No matter what expression a boy might assume, Bruce found it to be an affront. If the boy smiled it was surely a smirk, and if the boy frowned it demonstrated a surly attitude. Bruce could find reason to fight from the way a boy stood, slouched, or combed his hair. When Bruce was out on the street looking for a fight, he found fault in the way a boy said hello. . . . He believed he could win the world by beating it into submission.[5]

By age fourteen, during his first year with Yip Man, Lee had become one of the master's most promising students; he had also become obsessed with being number one someday. By the end of his second year, he advanced to the level of an intermediate student—a great leap in status in a very short period of time. One of his senior instructors recalls:

[The other students] were upset because he was progressing so fast. I noticed that, even when he was talking, he was always doing some kind of arm or leg movement. That's when I realized that he was actually serious about *kung fu*.[6]

EARLY LESSONS

From 1953 to 1958, Bruce Lee studied with Yip Man, the grand master of the kung fu style wing chun. *In one of Bruce Lee's early essays, published in Linda Lee's biography* The Bruce Lee Story, *Bruce Lee reflects on one of the early lessons he learned through his training.*

About four years of hard training in the art of gung fu [kung fu] I began to understand and felt the principle of gentleness—the art of neutralizing the effect of the opponent's effort and minimizing the expenditure of one's energy. All these must be done in calmness and without striving. It sounded simple, but in actual application it was difficult. . . . My instructor Professor Yip Man, head of the Wing Chun School, would come up to me and say, "Loong [dragon], relax and calm your mind. Forget about yourself and follow the opponent's movement without any interfering deliberation. Above all, learn the art of detachment."

The following week I stayed home. After spending many hours in meditation and practice, I gave up and went sailing alone in a junk. On the sea, I thought of all my past training and got mad at myself and punched the water. Right then at that moment, a thought suddenly struck me. Wasn't this water, the very basic stuff, the essence of gung fu? Didn't the common water just illustrate to me the principle of gung fu? I struck it just now, but it did not suffer hurt. Again, I stabbed it with all my might, yet it was not wounded. I then tried to grasp a handful of it but it was impossible. . . . Shouldn't it be the same then that the thoughts and emotions I had in front of an opponent [be] like the reflection of the bird over the water. This was exactly what Professor Yip Man meant by being detached—not being without emotion or feeling, but being one in whom feeling was not sticky or blocked.

Lee learned early the benefits of gentleness and detachment.

Chinese refugees flee Communist China. Unlike most Chinese, Lee could leave Hong Kong whenever he wanted to.

Expelled from La Salle for fighting in 1957, Lee enrolled at a new high school, the exclusive St. Francis Xavier College, in 1958. There, his reputation as a fighter continued to grow. "Bruce was king gorilla," Lee's younger brother Robert recalls. "Boss of the whole school." Even Yip Man said that Bruce was "fighting crazy."[7]

"WORTH HIS WEIGHT IN DIAMONDS"

The streets where Lee fought his battles were some of the most dangerous in the world at the time. After surviving the occupation by the Japanese, Hong Kong witnessed the tumultuous and dangerous years following the 1949 Communist triumph in mainland China. A constant stream of refugees, many fleeing Communist rule and famine conditions, poured into

Hong Kong. Shanty towns cropped up in the streets, crime escalated, and gangs of young men, both immigrants from the mainland and native Hong Kong Chinese, roamed the streets looking for trouble and adventure. Lee, with his temper, fearlessness, and fighting ability, was soon among the toughest. In a 1967 interview with *Black Belt* magazine, he said,

> I was a punk and went looking for fights. We used chains and pens with knives hidden inside them. . . . Kids [in Hong Kong] have nothing to look forward to. The white kids have all the best jobs and the rest of us had to work for them. That's why most of the kids become punks. Life in Hong Kong is so bad. Kids in slums can never get out.[8]

Lee was not really a slum kid, though. He was a special case and he knew it. He had his American citizenship waiting for him. In Hong Kong, usually only the very wealthy were able to emigrate, but Lee could emigrate anytime because he had been born in the United States. Tom Bleecker writes:

> To be a Chinese-American citizen living in Hong Kong in the 1940s–50s made Bruce Lee worth his weight in diamonds. In the final analysis, he didn't need school, and he didn't have to sidle up to anyone, be they family, friend, or foe.[9]

BOXING AND STREET FIGHTS

During his last year at St. Francis Xavier, one of Bruce Lee's teachers, a former boxer named Brother Edward, encouraged him to enter the 1958 Boxing Championship tournament, held among twelve Hong Kong high schools. Lee trained hard for the contest—working out, learning boxing footwork and punches—and his efforts paid off. He fought his way all the way through the preliminaries, leaving three opponents knocked out in the first round. In the final elimination fights, he faced the three-year champion. In the first rounds of the fight, Lee fought with usual boxing maneuvers, but his opponent was a superior boxer and Lee began to lose. Realizing that he could not beat his opponent by using traditional boxing methods, Lee changed tactics. He began fighting using his *wing chun* training. The strategy worked, and Lee won the fight.

Meanwhile, the street fights continued. Many martial arts teachers, Yip Man in-

cluded, encouraged students to try in real life what they learned in class. The various martial arts schools in Hong Kong conducted frequent and illegal contests on rooftops around Kowloon. The boys fought on rooftops in an attempt to stay out of view of the police, but the strategy did not always work. Grace Lee repeatedly found herself at the police station picking up her son.

In one of these fights, Lee lost his temper and not only beat up his opponent but knocked the boy down and beyond the boundary of the "ring," and then delivered two kicks to the boy's face, knocking out a tooth. The victim's parents went to the police and Grace was called to bail out her son again. Because of his repeated offenses and the severity of the beating, Grace had to sign a paper promising to take responsibility for his future conduct.

EXILED

After picking Lee up from the police station, Grace took him to lunch. She said nothing about the incident, but had a serious discussion with him about his future. She suggested that he leave Hong Kong, move to the United States, and claim his American citizenship. Lee replied that he did not want to leave home.

Fearing that her son would continue to fight and possibly end up in jail or dead, Grace went to her husband and convinced him to support her decision. Together, Lee's parents convinced Lee to leave home. Linda Lee writes: "All things considered, at that time in his life, Bruce never

A Quick Study

Bruce Lee often attributed his success in martial arts in part to his ability to focus quickly. In Bruce Lee: Fighting Spirit, *Bruce Thomas relates an anecdote demonstrating Bruce Lee's remarkable ability to learn quickly.*

Bruce told Hawkins Cheung [a childhood friend] that he was going to the United States to become a dentist, but then said he would earn money by teaching *kung fu*. Cheung reminded him that he only knew *wing chun* up to the second form. [Bruce] went to see a man known as Uncle Siu who taught northern styles of *kung fu* and . . . struck a deal with him: over the following months Siu would teach him some of his moves and in return, Bruce would give Siu dancing lessons. But Siu got the worst of the deal. He expected Bruce to take three or four weeks to learn the forms, when Bruce actually learned them in just three days—before Siu even got going with the basic cha-cha steps.

Bruce Lee demonstrates a difficult kung fu kick and shows his mastery of martial arts.

had any hope of gaining admission to college, and, had he stayed in Hong Kong, God only knows what might have become of him."[10]

Leaving his family, friends, and the only home he had ever known for the place of his birth was a thrilling but frightening prospect for eighteen-year-old Bruce Lee.

His parents gave him one hundred dollars and the name of friends in San Francisco with whom he could stay when he arrived. On April 29, 1959, Lee boarded a steamship bound for Tokyo, Honolulu, and San Francisco. He would not see Hong Kong or his parents again for more than four years.

2 The Seattle Years

Bruce Lee arrived in San Francisco, California, on May 17, 1959. When he stepped off the ship, Lee had only one hundred dollars in his pocket and the name of his father's friends in San Francisco with whom he was to stay. According to Linda Lee, Bruce Lee's first months in America were

> no tougher nor easier than it had been for millions of immigrants before him. Indeed, upon his arrival Bruce was already a citizen and possessed a rudimentary grasp of English, although he had to work hard to improve it.[11]

Lee's time in San Francisco was short-lived; he had trouble adapting to the city's Chinese community. Unhappy, he wrote to his mother, who arranged for him to go to Seattle, Washington, where another family friend would give him a job and a place to live. Lee moved to Seattle on September 3, 1959, and began his first steady job in America as a busboy in a Chinese restaurant.

RUBY CHOW'S

Ruby Chow's Chinese Restaurant, owned by Chow Ping and his wife Ruby, was on the outskirts of Seattle's International District.

Chow Ping was an old friend of Lee's father and a former fellow performer in the Cantonese opera. Chow Ping had fallen ill during the opera's 1940–1941 tour—the same tour during which Lee had been born—and

Shortly after arriving in America, Lee moved to Seattle, Washington (pictured).

Ruby Chow holds a bundle of Chinese long beans. Chow and her husband owned the Seattle restaurant where Lee worked as a busboy.

had been stranded in America when the United States declared war following the Japanese attack on Pearl Harbor. In San Francisco, Chow Ping met his future wife, Ruby, who nursed him back to health. The two married during World War II and moved to Seattle where they opened the restaurant.

Lee tried to fit into his new job at Ruby Chow's, but it was not easy. He did not get along with Ruby Chow, and she did not like him. She once said,

> If you can't say anything good about anyone, I'd rather not talk about it. . . . I took care of him [Bruce Lee] for four years and treated him like a second son. He was just not the sort of person you

want your children to grow up like—he was wild and undisciplined, he had no respect.[12]

For Lee, working for Ruby Chow was an enormous change from his life in Hong Kong. After years of doing as he pleased and never having to hold down a job or put in any effort at school, the menial work at the restaurant frustrated and angered him. He had assumed he had been sent to America to go to school and that he was to stay as Ruby Chow's guest. But that was not the reality.

Lee worked long days during his first years in Seattle. While living and working at Ruby Chow's, he enrolled at Edison Technical School, hoping to finish his high school diploma, and also took a second early morning job stuffing inserts into newspapers at the *Seattle Times* to make additional money. In a 1960 letter to a friend in Kowloon, Lee described his new life:

> At present I'm still going to the Edison High school, and will be graduated this summer. I plan to go to the University next year, that is, 1961. Well! I still don't know what I'm going to major in, but when I find out I'll write to you again. Now I find out that all those stuffs like Wing Chun . . . are just for killing time and have a little fun out of it, and that study always comes first. Yes, that's right, your own future depends on how well you have studied.
>
> Now I am really on my own. Since the day I stepped into this country, I didn't spend any money from my father. Now I am working as a waiter for a part time job after school. I'm telling you, it's tough, boy! I always have a heck of a time![13]

"YOU LOOK LIKE YOU CAN FIGHT"

Although he was determined to focus on school and spent many hours a day at work, Lee did not give up his kung fu practice. His continued practice made him quite adept, and he began giving lessons to other Chinese waiters in the parking lot of Ruby Chow's restaurant, in part to have others with whom to practice.

Lee also practiced at Edison Technical School, and several teachers took notice. In 1960, Seattle held an "Asian Culture Day," and the school administration asked Lee to put on a kung fu demonstration at the event. During the demonstration, Lee looked into the audience for a person to use as his "victim." One of the men in the audience was James DeMile, a former heavyweight boxing champion for the U.S. Air Force who had become a street fighter in a Seattle gang. Lee saw him and said, "You look like you can fight. How about coming up here?" Biographer Bruce Thomas describes what happened:

> DeMile looked every inch and every pound the fighter he was. He couldn't have been too worried as the young man beside him, who weighed 140 pounds and stood at five-foot-seven, explained that he was about to demonstrate a simple fighting system that had been devised by a tiny Buddhist nun. Bruce turned to DeMile and invited him to attack. DeMile fired out a straight right, intended to send [Bruce Lee's] head sailing over the crowd. Bruce blocked the punch easily as he countered simultaneously with his own punch that stopped a whisker away from DeMile's nose. From then on no matter what DeMile tried, Bruce was able to counter everything. . . . The demonstration continued without mercy, ending when Bruce knocked his knuckles against DeMile's head and asked if he was at home.[14]

The incident upset DeMile, but he approached Lee after the demonstration to ask if he could learn some *wing chun* techniques. Lee agreed to teach him.

Soon more and more interested students began showing up at the parking lot outside Ruby Chow's restaurant for lessons. This aggravated Ruby Chow because Lee often neglected or rushed through his chores as a busboy so that he could begin teaching his students. Ruby Chow would glare at Lee as he stood around outside talking with the students or when he invited a group inside the restaurant for something to eat. Lee, however, just glared back at her.

Although Lee never considered himself first and foremost a teacher, teaching did play a crucial role in his personal and professional life. Several of the men who came

AUNTIE RUBY

For four years, Bruce Lee lived in a room above Ruby Chow's Chinese Restaurant near the International District in Seattle. He also worked in the restaurant as a busboy—a job he hated. In Bruce Lee: The Biography, *director and biographer Robert Clouse describes some of the conflict between Lee and the restauranteur and matriarch Ruby Chow during those years.*

It was a smoking standoff for the couple of years Bruce spent there, but he was not the worst for the experience. When Bruce lived and worked in Ruby Chow's he had a room "no bigger than a closet." It was another reason he hated his life there. He had come from a rather well-to-do family in Hong Kong and now he was "less than a busboy" and treated in a like manner. He was used to being pampered. Top man. Here he was low man on a greased pole. He didn't like the way Ruby treated him, and, conversely, Ruby didn't like the way he treated her. She would say, "Bruce, you call me Auntie Ruby." Bruce would not do it. He would say, "You're no auntie of mine." And many times there would be a shouting match. Ruby expected the respect due to her, which is understood even more clearly in the Chinese culture, but Bruce would not succumb. . . . He felt Ruby was taking advantage of him. He believed he had been sent to Seattle to go to school and be Ruby's houseguest. No one had ever given Bruce a work schedule; Ruby was the first to ever really knock him down. She was unassailable as a wall. It was during that period that Bruce went from street punk to someone bent on making something of himself.

to study with Lee in the early days at Ruby Chow's ended up becoming his lifelong friends.

DRIVEN TO PERFECTION

As good at kung fu as he was, Bruce Lee never stopped pushing himself to improve, to perfect his techniques and learn new ones. He remained dedicated and obsessed with kung fu, and he spent most of his time thinking about it or practicing it. He began studying other martial arts such as karate and judo with Fook Young, an instructor at Seattle's Chinese Youth Club. He devoured books on martial arts and philosophy, scouring Seattle's numerous used bookstores for volumes, and in a short time he amassed a considerable library.

Attitude and positive thinking were important to Lee's martial arts practice. As he collected books on techniques and philosophy, Lee also became an avid reader of self-help books, an interest that lasted his entire adult life. Authors such as Norman Vincent Peale, Napoleon Hill, W. Clement Stone, Gyula Denes, and Maxwell Maltz were among his favorites.

Lee became seriously interested in self-improvement after having a dramatic nightmare. Throughout childhood and into adulthood, Lee had been prone to nightmares and sleepwalking. Robert Lee, Bruce Lee's brother, told of one night in 1959 when Bruce Lee, still asleep, sat up in bed, punching the covers as if fighting for his life. Bruce Lee said he had a nightmare in which he fought with what he described as a "black shadow." The shadow held him down, ren-

Lee enjoyed books by Norman Vincent Peale (pictured) and other self-help authors.

dering him helpless for several minutes. When he awoke, he was terrified, out of breath, and sweating profusely.

Because of Bruce Lee's sudden and seemingly mysterious death in 1973, numerous Lee filmmakers or biographers describe and dramatize this incident as a curse. Others say the shadow in his dream was a demon sent as a warning about his early death. Those who make these speculations about the dream use the incident as a tool to make their version of Lee's life seem supernatural and more dramatic. However, several biographers disagree, saying that the nightmare was just a dream—open to interpretation but not supernatural. One of these biographers, Bruce Thomas, writes:

Because it takes little imagination . . . to turn the event into a wild tale about a "demon" or a "curse," this has become the most cheapened and distorted incident of Bruce Lee's life. . . . That night, Bruce was not fighting a ghost but was being brought face-to-face with aspects of his personality that he had previously been reluctant to acknowledge: his anger, his cockiness, his insecurities. Bruce had simply met "himself." He underwent an intense confrontation with his own unconscious self, in which all the contradictions, the darker sides of his nature, were made apparent to him. It may very well have felt as if he were fighting a dark force. . . . Indeed, it was soon after this incident that Bruce Lee embarked on a course of serious self-improvement.[15]

GOALS

Whatever the meaning of the nightmare, Lee dedicated himself to what he considered the lifelong project of self-improvement. He defined and wrote out goals for himself—something he did for the rest of his life. These goals served as a challenge. Once he achieved a goal, he set another. He was never complacent and would never stop striving to improve.

One of the largest goals Lee set for himself was to spread knowledge of kung fu throughout the world. In a 1960 letter to a close family friend in Hong Kong, he describes his plan to achieve this goal:

Throughout his life, Bruce Lee set many goals for himself, including spreading knowledge of kung fu throughout the world.

I believe my long years of practice back up my title to become the first instructor of [the kung fu] movement [in America]. There are yet long years ahead of me to polish my techniques and character. My aim, therefore, is to establish a first Gung Fu [an alternate spelling of kung fu] Institute that will later spread out all over the U.S. (I have set a time limit of 10 to 15 years to complete the whole project). My reason in doing this is not the sole objective of making money. The motives are many and among them are: I would like to let the world know about the greatness of this Chinese art; I enjoy teaching and helping people; I like to have a well-to-do home for my family; I like to originate something; and the last but yet one of the most important is because gung fu is part of myself. . . . All in all, the goal of my planning and doing is to find the true meaning in life—peace of mind. I know that the sum of all possessions does not necessarily add up to peace of mind; however, it can be if I devote [my energy] to real accomplishment.[16]

DRAGON IN LOVE

Although Lee worked toward his goals with drive and tenacity, there were parts of his life that he could not so easily command. The most unpredictable of these was love.

He had been very popular with girls in Hong Kong, but it was harder for him to meet girls in America because of language and cultural differences. Thus, he tried to impress girls with his strength or martial arts ability, often using his kung fu demonstrations as an excuse to take off his shirt and show off his physique. Lee has said that one of his strategies for meeting girls was to wait for one to pass by the demonstration, pull one of his bigger students out of the class—usually James DeMile—and then beat him up to impress the girl. Despite all these strategies though, Lee's first girlfriend in America was not impressed by this approach.

Lee met Amy Sanbo at the University of Washington (UW). He graduated from Edison Technical School in the winter of 1960 and enrolled at UW in the spring of 1961. One day while sitting in the student

Lee met his first American girlfriend, Amy Sanbo, at the University of Washington (pictured).

union building, he saw Sanbo, an attractive Japanese American woman, and decided he wanted to meet her. Lee's first meeting with Sanbo did not go well, however. Sanbo describes that first encounter:

I kept noticing this Asian fellow kept moving . . . closer and closer to where [Sanbo and her friends] were sitting. Anyway, I had to go to class and so I was walking past him and he suddenly reached up and grabbed my arm and with his thumb he pressed with such force I thought I was going to die and my knees buckled and I dropped all my books on the floor. . . . I asked him why he had grabbed me like that, and he said he was just showing his friend something or other. I had no idea what he was saying. I was just in pain. . . . And I thought to myself, "What a complete jerk!"[17]

Over the next few weeks, Lee tried to improve on his first impression. He approached Sanbo repeatedly, introducing himself, asking how she was, and using any excuse to make conversation. Lee's persistence and kindness softened Sanbo's dislike for him. Sanbo continues:

I had hurt my ankle . . . and as a result had to walk on crutches for a week, and in order to get to school in the morning I had to walk . . . up this unbelievable flight of 367 concrete stairs north of the football stadium. . . . And then one morning Bruce appeared, picked me up off my feet and carried me, my books, my crutches, and my heavy coat all the way to the top of those stairs. . . .

And he did this every day, for the entire week I was on crutches. And it wasn't only those stairs. After school he carried me to the third floor of my apartment and anywhere else he thought would be a problem for me.[18]

Lee fell in love with Sanbo, and she eventually came to like him very much. She was attracted to his charm and unusual confidence. "More than anything else," she said, "what I liked most about Bruce was that he never apologized for being Oriental. Back then most of the Asian fellows did apologize. . . . Bruce was so cocky that it was refreshing."[19]

HEARTBREAK

Although Lee and Sanbo got along for a while, Sanbo found Lee's personality aggravating. Although he was kind when they were alone, he was arrogant and openly chauvinistic in public. Sanbo thought Lee was self-centered. He often dominated conversations with his favorite subjects: kung fu, himself, and his plans for the future. "There was an awful lot of stuff that came out of his mouth that was just plain insufferable,"[20] Sanbo said.

Lee proposed marriage to Sanbo again and again, but she continually turned him down. Sanbo had ambitions to become a writer and a dancer, and Lee held very traditional Chinese values about marriage. By Chinese custom, women were expected to be only wives, mothers, and homemakers.

The three-year relationship ended in early 1963. Sanbo did not want to marry

BRUCE "SIFU" LEE MEETS THEODORE ROETHKE

In Tom Bleecker's biography, Unsettled Matters: The Life and Death of Bruce Lee, *Amy Sanbo, Bruce Lee's first girlfriend in America, recalls Lee's unflappable confidence and charm when he met Pulitzer Prize–winning poet Theodore Roethke in a classroom at the University of Washington.*

Bruce and I [were] sitting alone studying in Roethke's classroom at the University. Now you have to understand that Theodore Roethke was the only instructor in the English department who actually had his own classroom. And so in walks Roethke—a man so huge that he often described himself as a bear in his poems—and he says, "I'm Roethke, the poet! You're in my room!" I was in total shock and I thought, "Roethke, my god!" And I was enough of a student to back off and think, "Okay, I'll bow down. I'll keep quiet." But Bruce didn't flinch at all. He stood up and walked right up to Roethke and stuck out his hand and said, "I'm Bruce

Sifu (teacher) Lee," with the emphasis on *Sifu, "Kung-fu* master." My god, I was ready to crawl out under the door, and I was hoping that Roethke hadn't caught a good glimpse of me. I guess I was in a daze for a while, and then the next thing I remember is looking up and seeing Bruce standing at the blackboard with chalk in his hand, lecturing to Roethke who is sitting in a front row chair! And Bruce is explaining to this Pulitzer Prize winning poet the essentials of *kung fu* and he's drawing Chinese characters all over Roethke's blackboard. And so for the next half-hour I stood there absolutely fascinated watching Bruce Lee captivate, if not mesmerize, Theodore Roethke and thinking, "Oh my god, this is totally and completely bizarre!"

Theodore Roethke, Pulitzer Prize winner and professor at the University of Washington.

Lee, so she broke up with him. Lee would not accept that the relationship was over and continued to pursue her after the breakup. He was so persistent that when Sanbo left Seattle to take a job in New York that summer, she told her family not to let Lee know where she was living. Heartbroken, Lee decided to return to Hong Kong to visit his family.

LINDA

When Bruce Lee went to Hong Kong during the summer of 1963, it was the first time in four years that he had seen his home and parents. When he arrived, his father was impressed by the transformation of his rebellious and troublesome teenage son into a successful young man.

Lee was happy to be among his old friends and family, and he spent the summer having fun with Doug Palmer, a friend and kung fu student who accompanied him on the trip. He also softened the blow of his breakup with Sanbo by having a short affair with a childhood friend, Pak Yan. The reunion with his parents and Hong Kong friends was therapeutic for Lee, and he left Hong Kong in better spirits.

Returning to Seattle in August, Lee resumed classes and kung fu instruction. Lee's popularity as an instructor grew. He attracted new students through demonstrations on campus and by word of mouth. Eventually, he was teaching as many as a

MISCHIEF IN HONG KONG

Doug Palmer, a friend and student of Bruce Lee's from the University of Washington, went to Hong Kong with Lee in the summer of 1964. During their visit, Lee and Palmer amused themselves by playing practical jokes on locals. Quoted in Bruce Thomas's biography, Bruce Lee: Fighting Spirit, *Palmer describes one of their pranks, played on Hong Kong police officers.*

Once we spotted one of the cops with a red bar [meaning the officer spoke at least rudimentary English], my job was to walk up to him and ask if he could tell me the way to the Canton Theatre. Since there was no Canton Theatre, but there was a Canton Road, the cop would invariably ask, in heavily accented English, "Canton Road?" "No!" I'd say I was supposed to meet a friend at the Canton Theatre and, thereupon, I would launch into a nonstop monologue of double-talk. Each time the confused cop would repeat, "Canton Road?" I would give another burst of double-talk. Finally, I would demand loudly, in Cantonese, "What the hell are you mumbling about?" At that point, Bruce would stroll up helpfully and ask what the problem was. I would explain that I was looking for the Canton Theatre. Bruce would say that he was going that way and we would walk off leaving the cop with an even more confused look on his face.

Bruce Lee and his wife Linda pose for a photographer. They met at Lee's Jun Fan Gung Fu Institute.

dozen students at a time. Because his student base was growing so quickly, one of his students and friends, Taky Kimura, suggested that Lee collect a small fee from each of his students. With the money, he could open a studio of his own and quit his job at Ruby Chow's. Lee agreed and, in late 1963, opened the Jun Fan Gung Fu Institute in a neighborhood near the university. He set up a bedroom in a small windowless room in the back of the studio, furnishing it with Chinese items brought back from his summer in Hong Kong.

One of his first new students at his studio was eighteen-year-old Linda Emery. Emery had come to the class mostly to meet Lee, whom she had seen months before when he had given a talk on Chinese philosophy at her high school. She thought he was very good-looking and signed up for kung fu classes so she could meet him. She did not expect to like the class, but to her surprise, she enjoyed learning kung fu.

Emery got to know Lee over the first weeks of kung fu classes. Lee and his students spent almost every weekday afternoon together, practicing kung fu, eating Chinese food, and going to movies. The more she got to know Lee, the more she liked about him. He was an impressive martial artist, a generous teacher, and a funny, charming man. She developed a crush on him, but did not entertain hopes that he was attracted to her because he did not seem to give her any more attention than he gave the rest of his students. Linda Lee recalls how surprised she was when he asked her out on a date:

I didn't think Bruce would ever consider me romantically. . . . He was so dashing and charming, he could have had his choice of dates. Regardless, I was having fun being part of the kung fu group. One of our favorite things to do at school was to go over to the large, rectangular grass area used for outdoor

A DATE AT THE TOP OF THE CITY

In The Bruce Lee Story, *Linda Lee describes her first date with Bruce Lee.*

Bruce picked me up in his black '57 Ford at my girlfriend's house. My mom would have never let me go out with him alone so I just skirted that issue for the time being. I had borrowed my friend's dress and coat because I didn't have anything appropriate to wear to a fancy restaurant. . . . Class was the word for Bruce. When he arrived for our date he was wearing a black Italian silk suit, purple shirt, and black tie. His hair was slicked back on the sides and a curl dangled on his forehead. He looked so much like my idol George Chakaris, the leader of the Sharks in *West Side Story*, that I was instantly charmed.

I was nervous about being able to carry on a conversation with this gorgeous man now that I was alone with him and did not have the security of a group. . . . My fears were needless, however, as Bruce put me completely at ease. He always could talk enough for the both of us, and even in later years, whenever I was at a loss for words, he would fill in the gaps. Over dinner, I was fascinated with Bruce's life story and with his plans for the future. In my mind it occurred to me to ask him why he had singled me out for this romantic dinner, but I was too shy to bring it up. To complete the evening, Bruce presented me with a memento. It was a tiny Scandinavian troll doll, a kewpie doll. Bruce had gone to the trouble of braiding its hair into pigtails. I was delighted because I knew instantly the significance of the gift. It looked just like me when I would walk into the Student Union Building with wet hair in pigtails after my swimming class. Bruce was the best gift-giver—he always gave the personal touch when he didn't have the money as well as when he could afford to be more lavish. Our date ended with a light kiss when Bruce dropped me off at my house. It was the end of a perfect evening.

concerts [at the University of Washington]. It was fenced-in by trees and by beautiful Grecian columns on one end. The whole group of us would go there to practice *kung fu* with plenty of space and soft grass to land on. One afternoon, Bruce and I were racing from one end to the other and when we got away from the group he tackled me to the ground. I thought he was going to show me a new maneuver, but instead he held me down and when I stopped laughing, he asked me if I wanted to go to dinner at the Space Needle. I hesitated a moment, thinking that was a pretty expensive place for [the whole class] to go, and I said, "You mean all of us?" And he replied, "No, only you and me." I was speechless, although I must have managed to say, "Yes!"[21]

Bruce Lee began dating Linda Emery. They spent as much time together as they could, and over the following weeks they fell in love. However, Emery had to keep their relationship a secret from her mother, who was against interracial relationships. Emery had previously dated a Japanese American classmate, and her mother had made her break up with him. Emery was falling in love with Lee and did not want to risk the same thing happening with this relationship. She writes:

Since [my mother] did not know I was dating Bruce, it was getting to be a sticky situation and I was at a loss as to how to handle it. I didn't like deceiving my mom but I liked even less the idea of not being able to see Bruce, and I knew she had very strong feelings about that subject. It was one of those issues in life for which there is no satisfactory solution and so I put it on the back burner for the time. Since Bruce and I were almost constantly together, it took quite a bit of maneuvering and a little help from my friends.[22]

Lying to her mother was only one of the problems brought about by her relationship with Lee. Because she was spending so much time with Lee rather than schoolwork, Emery's studies began to suffer. Meanwhile, Lee had become a competent

but undirected student. He took whatever courses interested him rather than planning a degree program. As a result, he did not have the appropriate credits to advance to the sophomore level after three years of study. By the end of his third year, he decided to quit the university.

LEAVING HOME AGAIN

The Jun Fan Gung Fu Institute was having trouble also. Because of a high turnover of students, the monthly dues were not enough for Lee to pay the rent. But Lee would never admit failure. He decided to go to Oakland, California, to stay with James Lee (no relation), another kung fu practitioner whom he had met years earlier. Lee hoped the two of them could open a second kung fu school in Oakland while Taky Kimura, one of his assistant instructors, ran the first school in Seattle. Lee made his plans and acted on them immediately. He sold his car and shipped all of his belongings to Oakland.

While all of this was going on, Lee did not talk to Emery about how he felt about leaving her. Emery knew that Lee's martial arts goals were the most important thing to him, and that his plans to further those goals were not open for debate or questioning. However, as she watched him prepare to leave, Emery wondered to herself what would happen to their relationship. She recalls:

I watched this whirlwind of activity with trepidation, wondering how I fit into the master plan. When I took

Bruce to the airport for his departure, I still didn't know the answer to that question. Neither did Bruce. The idea of commitment scared him to death. He wanted to be financially secure before undertaking the responsibility of a wife and family. We talked about marriage, but later, some distant time down the road. As he got ready to board the plane, Bruce could read the feelings on my face. He said simply, "I'll be back," and then he was gone. I felt like the bottom had dropped out of my life.[23]

When he left Seattle, as when he had left Hong Kong, Lee left behind his friends and familiar surroundings. In August 1963, he arrived in Oakland with little more than his ambitions and his goals.

Chapter

3 Discovered!

Bruce Lee moved in with James Lee and his family in Oakland, California, in the summer of 1964. James Lee was a well-known kung fu instructor and practitioner in the Chinese community. Biographer Robert Clouse describes James Lee:

> [James Lee] always appeared disheveled and his hair uncombed even when it was, and his clothes were rather ill-fitting. His specialty was "iron-hand techniques," breaking bricks or boards. Many of his techniques were so often considered stunts, and "fake stunts," but he could do them. He could do just what he said he could do, which always appealed to Bruce. Bruce hated frauds and celebrated those who could "produce."[24]

James Lee and Bruce Lee had met during Bruce Lee's days of teaching in Ruby Chow's parking lot. Over the years, they corresponded frequently, discussing kung fu and philosophy. Many biographers assert that James Lee became a father figure to Bruce Lee, who had only a distant relationship with his real father. Certainly Bruce Lee trusted and liked James Lee, and on July 19, 1964, they opened the second Jun Fan Gung Fu Institute in Oakland's Chinatown.

MAKING AN IMPRESSION

To gather support and recognition for his new school in Oakland, Bruce Lee appeared at the International Karate Tournament in Long Beach, California, on August 2, 1964. The tournament was one of the nation's largest martial arts events, established and sponsored by Ed Parker, one of the most important American figures in karate. Although kung fu was not a well-known martial arts style (especially outside the Chinese community), Ed Parker allowed Lee to demonstrate at the tournament. Lee impressed Parker with his innovative ideas about martial arts. Although many martial arts practitioners follow prescribed rules and forms, Parker says he liked the fact that Lee was

> very broad-minded about things—very anti-classical . . . he felt [classical practitioners] were all robots. So I told him that if he were to come down to the tournament and demonstrate, people would have a better cross section of the martial arts world.[25]

To impress the audience, Lee gave a demonstration of his one-inch punch, a technique in which a punch began a distance of

MY CHIEF PERSONAL AIM IN LIFE

Bruce Lee was an ambitious man who consistently laid out and pursued very specific goals. In his book Unsettled Matters: The Life and Death of Bruce Lee, *biographer Tom Bleecker quotes a passage written by Bruce Lee during his early career, following* The Green Hornet, *that describes his vision for his future.*

I, Bruce Lee, will be the highest paid Oriental superstar in the United States. In return I will give the most exciting performances and render the best quality in the capacity of an actor. Starting in 1970, I will achieve world fame and from then onward till the end of 1980 I will have in my possession the sum of $10,000,000—then I will live the way I please and achieve inner harmony and happiness.

Bruce Lee flexes on a film set.

only an inch from the opponent's chest and could send a man three times Lee's size flying backward. Lee did not like to use tricks or stunts unless there was an instructive principle behind them. Thus he used the one-inch punch to get the audience's attention, and then he could explain the philosophy behind the trick. As Bruce Thomas explains:

> The real purpose of the inch-punch was to show that there is a far more powerful way of striking someone than simply using the strength of the arm and shoulder muscles. The more relaxed the muscles are, the more energy can flow through the body. Using muscular tension to try to "do" the punch or attempting to use brute force to knock someone over will only work to opposite effect.[26]

With his goal of spreading awareness of kung fu, Lee also used the tournament to show off his fighting style. He challenged Dan Inosanto, a formidable Filipino *kenpo* karate master, to be his opponent in a demonstration. Lee told Inosanto to attack with everything he had. Inosanto recalls the fight:

> I was completely flabbergasted! He controlled me like a baby—I couldn't do anything with him at all. He didn't have to use much force either—he just sort of body-controlled me. I'd lost to other people before but not in the way that I lost to him: he was dominating the action completely, calling the shots like it was a game! I couldn't sleep that night. It seemed as though everything I'd done in the past was obsolete—he countered everything I knew without really trying. It was very frustrating.[27]

Inosanto went back to Lee's hotel room after the match and the two men traded ideas and techniques. Lee always enjoyed meeting serious martial artists, and Inosanto was eager to learn from the man who had so easily defeated him. The two began a lifelong friendship. Inosanto became one of Lee's first students at the new school and eventually became an assistant instructor.

There was someone else in the audience at the Long Beach tournament whose presence changed the course of Lee's career. Jay Sebring, owner of a Beverly Hills hair salon, came to the tournament and, with the rest of the audience, sat mesmerized as he watched Lee perform.

Sebring had never seen anyone like Lee. His abilities seemed almost miraculous, and the performance left a lasting impression on Sebring. Sebring's salon catered to many Hollywood celebrities and filmmakers. One client was television producer William Dozier, who had produced such series as *Gunsmoke* and *Perry Mason*. When Dozier mentioned to Sebring that his studio, Twentieth-Century Fox, was looking for a young Asian actor for a role in a new television series, Sebring suggested that Dozier get in touch with Bruce Lee.

THE SUMMER OF LETTERS

At the same time that Lee's professional life was about to take a significant turn toward fame, his personal life was also about to transform. Linda Emery's worries that Lee would forget about her when he left for California proved unfounded. The two

Twentieth-Century Fox producer, William Dozier (pictured), first heard about Lee from hair salon owner Jay Sebring.

exchanged letters almost daily while Lee was gone, and their relationship continued to strengthen in spite of the distance.

On August 12, 1964, Lee returned to Seattle to propose. Emery accepted, but there were obstacles to overcome before they could marry. Linda Lee writes:

> There was the problem of my family, especially of my mom. This was going to be a very delicate situation full of anger and hurt. Bruce was very concerned about my family's reaction. In fact, it was one of the reasons he had hesitated so long. He realized even better than I did, that when you marry a woman, you marry the family as well. He didn't want to enter our marriage with the

black cloud of rejection hanging over us. But we had ducked this issue for so long now that it was very complicated. Being young and in love, however, love won out, and we decided to face the music. I felt terrible about it, but I knew that marrying Bruce was the right thing to do. Bruce and I decided on the coward's way out. We'd get married, run away to Oakland, then call my mom and tell her. . . . We went to the King County Courthouse [in Washington State] to apply for a marriage license. Aside from the mandatory three-day waiting period, there was one major problem we hadn't foreseen. . . . [W]e didn't know that all the names of those who apply for marriage licenses are published in the newspaper.[28]

Emery's aunt read the announcement in the newspaper and called Emery's mother to complain about not being invited to the wedding. Surprised and angry, Emery's mother called several relatives in Washington and arranged for a family meeting to confront Emery and Lee (whom none of them had met) to convince them to change their minds about getting married.

A DAY OF TEARS

At the meeting, Emery's family, including her mother, stepfather, aunt, uncle, and grandmother, sat in the living room of her house. They made it clear that they were against the marriage. They had never met Lee, so it was not a matter of them disliking him. However, the family was not happy that Lee was Chinese. Linda Lee writes:

The big issue was the interracial aspect. They felt we would suffer the slings and arrows of society's prejudice, and our children likewise. My aunt and uncle were very religious and they thought the mixing of the races was an abomination.[29]

In spite of the opposition from Emery's family, Bruce Lee was not one to let others get in the way of what he wanted. His own mother was half Caucasian, something that had not always been easy to live with in Hong Kong's traditional Chinese society, so he was not unfamiliar with racism. Before going to meet Emery's family, he decided that he would be polite and nice to the family but that he was not going to back down. At the meeting, he smiled and introduced himself to Emery's mother, saying, "I want to marry your daughter. We are leaving on Monday [to

As a biracial person of Asian and Caucasian lineage, Lee faced discrimination and racism throughout life.

return to Oakland]. I'm Chinese, by the way."[30]

Besides their commitment to each other, there was another big reason for the couple to marry: Emery was pregnant. That ended the argument. The family unhappily consented to the marriage, hastily arranging a wedding for August 17, the next day. Instead of a happy day, the wedding was marred by ill feelings. Emery's mother felt betrayed because Emery had hidden her relationship with Lee for so long, and she maintained prejudice against interracial marriage even as her daughter married Lee. Linda Lee describes her wedding day as "a perfectly horrible day. This was the day of tears."[31]

Taky Kimura, posing by Bruce Lee's gravesite, was Bruce's best man in his wedding.

The ceremony was held in the Seattle Congregational Church; a minister hired on short notice presided. Taky Kimura acted as best man and Emery's mother and grandmother acted as witnesses. Emery wore a brown dress and there were no flowers.

In spite of the troubles over the announcement and the wedding, Linda Lee thinks positively about the beginning of her marriage to Bruce Lee. She writes:

> Looking back on the wedding, one might think that because of all this turmoil our marriage got off to an inauspicious beginning. I believe it only served to strengthen our resolve to make this union work. By questioning us so thoroughly and making us explain our feelings for each other out loud, my family actually served as premarriage counselors.[32]

GOING AGAINST TRADITION

The newlyweds left Seattle for Oakland the day after the ceremony and moved into James Lee's household. Soon after, James Lee's wife developed cancer and died, leaving him with two young children to care for. Bruce and Linda Lee helped James Lee care for the kids, and Linda learned to cook three meals a day for a household of five.

Soon after Bruce and Linda Lee arrived in Oakland, trouble also arose at the new kung fu school. Because Bruce Lee believed in merit rather than race, his schools were open to any able and sincere student. This made many Asian practitioners angry since until this time, kung fu had never been

BRUCE LEE ON MARRIAGE

Married in 1964, Bruce and Linda Lee maintained a strong marriage until Bruce's death. In a 1971 interview with the Hong Kong newspaper The China Mail, *published in* Bruce Lee: Words of the Dragon *(edited by John Little), Bruce Lee spoke about his philosophies on marriage and speculated about why he and Linda were so happy.*

I am a fortunate man. I am fortunate not because my film can break a record, but because I have a good wife, Linda. She is unsurpassed. Why do I say this? First, I believe, a couple should develop a kind of friendship. We understand each other, like a pair of good friends. We thus can stay happily together. The quality in Linda that moves me is her neutral love for me. She treats our relationship with calmness, objectivity, and neutrality. I think this is the kind of attitude that a couple should adopt. For example, if I state a point, my wife has her idea. Certainly we ought to discuss things or it would be difficult for us to get along well. The happiness we have today is built on the ordinary life we had before we married. The happiness that is got from ordinary life can last longer: like coal, it burns gradually and slowly. The happiness that is got from the excitement is like a brilliant fire—soon it will go out. Before we married, we never had the chance to go to nightclubs. We only spent our nights watching TV and chatting. Many young couples live a very exciting life when they are in love. So, when they marry, and their lives are reduced to calmness and dullness, they will feel very impatient and will drink the bitter cup of a sad marriage.

taught to Westerners. In China, secret societies practicing kung fu and other martial arts formed as a means of resisting outsiders such as the colonial British in Hong Kong. Because Westerners were usually taller and stronger than Asians, martial arts became a way to even the odds for the Asians. To preserve that advantage, the Asians kept kung fu techniques secret from Westerners. Lee considered this way of thinking to be outdated. He felt that if a Westerner wanted to hurt an Asian, the Westerner did not need kung fu to do it. "After all," he said, "[the white man]'s bigger."[33]

SHOWDOWN

In September 1964, several martial arts schools in San Francisco sent a representative, Wong Jack Man, to Lee's school with a challenge. Wong was a formidable fighter. He and several other fighters from his

Lee's willingness to introduce Westerners to martial arts, both at his school and in films, raised much opposition from traditional Asian martial artists.

school demanded that Lee stop teaching the sacred and secret Chinese fighting methods to foreigners. If Lee refused to abide by the demand, Wong would fight him in a showdown. If Lee lost the fight, he would have to close his school.

As stubborn and determined as he had been as a youth, Lee refused to back down and accepted the challenge. Linda Lee describes what happened:

> Obviously [the challengers] thought that Bruce was a paper tiger, who, faced with an actual challenge by a skilled

practitioner would simply chicken out. [Nervous, Wong and his friends] suggested to Bruce, "Let's not make this a match—let's just spar together. Let's just try out our techniques."

Bruce swept this aside impatiently and angrily. Few men had a quicker temper. "No, you challenged me. So let's fight!"[34]

Wong tried to establish some rules for the fight but Lee refused to listen. He told Wong that if they fought it would be without rules—all out. The two men bowed and began to fight. Within three minutes, Lee had defeated Wong. To make sure there was no dispute over his victory, Lee made Wong declare his defeat aloud before Lee would let him up. He physically threw Wong out of the school and made Wong's friends leave the premises.

The story of the fight got around the community and no one gave Lee or the school trouble again. "In fact," Linda Lee continues, "if you go into San Francisco's Chinatown today—or any other Chinatown—you'll find that Bruce is the great hero."[35]

NEW DIRECTION

After the showdown, Lee reflected on the fight and was disappointed and angry with himself. Although he had beaten Wong Jack Man in only three minutes, Lee was upset by his performance in the fight. Although tournament fights and boxing matches last much longer, Lee knew that street fights

---

GETTING FIT

Shaken by his showdown with a fighter representing rival martial arts schools from San Francisco, Bruce Lee embarked on an intensive fitness regime in 1964 to improve his skills. In Bruce Lee: Fighting Spirit, *Bruce Thomas describes the program undertaken by Lee.*

[Bruce] started every day with an early morning run of several miles, often with Bobo, the Great Dane. For Bruce, running was also a kind of meditation, an opportunity to let things flow. Houses, cars, and trees passed along with his thoughts. . . . After lunch there was another run or an hour on the exercise bike.

Conditioning exercises centered mainly on the abdomen, using the tried-and-tested boxing method of having a heavy medicine ball thrown at his midsection, along with sit-ups and leg raises. . . .

James [Lee] also started Bruce on weight training. At first he did reverse curls all day to develop his forearms, but once he had seen how it might add strength to his speed he bought a full set of weights and used them consistently. Bruce did everything he could to maintain his muscular gains and also began experimenting with high-protein weight-gain drinks that he blended himself and supplemented with ginseng, royal jelly, and massive doses of vitamins. Once committed to a course of action, Bruce would take it to the limit. His workout schedule listed the number of repetitions of the exercises he had set himself to do: beside some was the note "INF"—meaning "to infinity." He would keep going until he could go no further—and then keep going!

---

should be over as quickly as possible. Three minutes was too long. He began to doubt his practice techniques and his ability. He had not been in a fight outside of a class or tournament since he left Hong Kong. Up to this time, Lee had been happy with his practice, which included primarily *wing chun* and some variations from other styles. But the showdown proved to him that what he was doing was not good enough. Not only that, but the fight had winded him, demonstrating that he was not in as good condition as he thought.

Always a student and perfectionist, Lee learned from the experience and set about a rigorous training schedule to get into better fighting condition. He took vitamins, royal jelly, and ginseng to speed his metabolism and build strength. In addition to his daily kung fu training, he also began running two to six miles each morning, then covering ten to twenty miles on a stationary bicycle in the afternoon.

Lee also began designing new training equipment that would mimic the unpredictability of human opponents and increase his speed. James Lee was a welder by trade, and along with another student, Herb Jackson, an expert and innovative craftsman, he built the equipment Bruce Lee designed. Among Lee's designs were forearm developers, sparring shields, spring-action and wall-mounted punching bags, and padded body suits to allow full-contact sparring.

GOOD NEWS AND MORE GOOD NEWS

One afternoon while Bruce Lee was training, Linda Lee received a phone call. It was television producer William Dozier. Dozier had seen a film of Bruce Lee's demonstration at the International Karate Championships. He liked what he saw and wanted Lee to come to Hollywood to do a screen test for a role in a new television series based on an old radio program called *Charlie Chan*.

Lee was thrilled when he heard the news and immediately agreed to fly to Los Angeles in the first week of February. Three days before the screen test, on February 1, 1965, Linda Lee gave birth to Brandon Bruce Lee. Like his father, Brandon was born in the Chinese Year of the Dragon, considered the most auspicious year in the Chinese zodiac.

SCREEN TEST

Bruce Lee walked into Twentieth-Century Fox Studios in Hollywood for his screen test on February 4, 1965. His natural charm and screen presence were apparent from the start. He joked about the loss of sleep over his new baby and began talking about his favorite subject, kung fu. He told stories, explained kung fu techniques, and then asked for a volunteer to help him with a demonstration. Bruce Thomas says:

> A man with silver hair and spectacles, one of the studio staff, was "volunteered" to the delight of his snickering colleagues. . . .
>
> "There are various kinds of fights," he [Lee] began. "It depends on where you hit and what weapon you will be using. To the eyes you will use the fingers."

Bruce threw a lightning . . . strike towards the man's eyes. The old man looked more than worried. "Don't worry," Bruce assured him, and whipped out another jab to his eyes. "And to the face," added Bruce as his punches made an audible rush of air, lashing within an inch of the man's nose. . . .

The subdued chuckles from the floor became belly laughs and Bruce joined in the conspiracy with the studio technicians, trying to hide the laughter with his hand across his face. . . .

"You know kung fu is very sneaky," Bruce said, "just like the Chinese."[76]

Next, Lee moved into demonstrations of various techniques, adding flourished high kicks to give a good show. When he finished, the director came forward and shook his hand, very pleased by the performance.

BAD NEWS AND MORE BAD NEWS

A week later, Bruce Lee's father Li Hoi Chuen died in Hong Kong, and Lee flew back alone to attend the funeral. Chinese tradition dictates that when a son is not present at his father's death he must do penance because the absence is considered disrespectful to the father. The son must make amends to his father's spirit by crawling to the deathbed or casket on his hands and knees. Lee crawled from the front door of the funeral home to his father's coffin, wailing loudly for the benefit of his family and onlookers. Lee's relationship with his father had been a difficult and distanced one, but he loved his father and publicly mourned him.

Lee spent two weeks in Hong Kong. When he returned to Oakland, Dozier called with more bad news. Although Lee had won the studio over and had been the favorite choice for the *Charlie Chan* series, the studio decided not to produce the television show. However, there was a new series in the works called *The Green Hornet*, based on an old radio serial program featuring a superhero crime fighter. The studio executives wanted to cast Lee in the role of Kato, the Green Hornet's sidekick. The producers were waiting to start filming, though, because they wanted to see the audience response to another new superhero television series called *Batman*. If the response to *Batman* was good, *The Green Hornet* would begin production; if it was bad, the project would be called off.

Lee signed a one-year option contract for eighteen hundred dollars. The contract guaranteed that the role of Kato would be his if the series deal came through. If the series was not produced, he could keep the money—and eighteen hundred dollars was more money than Lee had seen in a long time.

FAMILY MATTERS

To celebrate the option contract, Lee and his family boarded a plane for Hong Kong in May 1965. Lee's plan was that he, Linda, and Brandon would spend four months in Hong Kong with his mother and siblings, then

DEAR LINDA

Li Hoi Chuen, Bruce Lee's father, died on February 8, 1965. While in Hong Kong for his father's funeral, a homesick Bruce wrote many letters to his wife Linda. This letter, dated February 15, 1965, appears in Bruce Lee: Letters of the Dragon: Correspondence, 1958–1973 *(edited by John Little), and it demonstrates Bruce Lee's affection and concern for his wife and son. Lee was a new husband and father and worried about his family's health and happiness while he was away.*

Linda,

I'm most comforted to receive your letter, especially at a time like this. The whole family is in a state of sadness and confusion. . . .

One thing I'm anxious about is your health and secondly my son Brandon. I hope you will go have a check up and bring Brandon boy along, too. Never mind about the expense, your health is more important. Any amount you need will be okay with me. If you're short of cash get it from mother and I'll reimburse whatever the amount. . . .

By the time this letter reaches you I might have given you a phone call already—I do not know yet because all money and property are tied up until the reading of the will. . . .

In the meantime, you must take good care of yourself and Brandon. Do not forget about the doctor and above all do not forget to let me know of the result (like your blood count, etc.) If there is anything that has to be done, do it! (like Brandon's shots or anything) Do not worry about expenses. I'll be able to pay for it.

Take good care of yourself and Brandon boy.
With all my love,
Bruce

---

they would return to America and spend four more months with Linda's mother and stepfather in Seattle. Afterward, they would move to Los Angeles. Lee felt certain that *The Green Hornet* deal would come through.

The trip to Hong Kong was difficult for Linda. Although Bruce's family was kind and accepted the couple's interracial marriage, Linda spoke almost no Chinese and Bruce's family almost no English. To make matters worse, Brandon was fussy—he was not used to the humidity and heat of Hong Kong. Further, as Chinese custom dictated, Bruce's mother Grace and sister Agnes immediately picked up Brandon if he began to fuss or cry. Because she was trying to fit in and be accepted by Bruce's family, Linda had to try to get to Brandon first so that she would not lose the family's respect. As a result, she got very little sleep and soon became irritable and weary.

Wanting to show off his new bride to his family, Bruce also bragged about Linda's cooking, even though she was still just learning. He told them that she could make the best spaghetti dinner in the world, which was far from true. Linda Lee writes:

Bruce's family was excited about trying it. I was on the spot! My first problem was finding the right ingredients, not an easy trick in a city that didn't have supermarkets as we know them in the United States. . . . A feeling of dread came over me. I managed to get some semblance of ingredients together. . . . A huge crowd was gathering in the apartment, as relatives from far and near assembled for this special event. The most I had ever cooked for was five, and now there were at least 25 people preparing for this alleged feast. My next problem was that I had never used a gas stove and I didn't

In his first role for American television, Lee (left) played Kato, sidekick to the Green Hornet (right).

BRANDON LEE AND THE CURSE OF *THE CROW*

Years after Bruce Lee's untimely death, his son Brandon Lee also became an actor and martial artist. In 1993, while working on the set of what was meant to be his breakthrough film, The Crow, *Brandon was killed in an accident. In her April 7, 2000,* Entertainment Weekly *article written seven years after his death, Erin Richter describes the incident.*

The Crow seemed born under its own curse. . . . From its very first day, when a carpenter suffered severe burns after his crane hit the power lines, the 58-day shoot in Wilmington, N.C., was besieged with troubles. . . . [A] grip truck caught fire, a disgruntled sculptor crashed his car through the studio's plaster shop, and a crew member accidentally drove a screwdriver through his hand. The already stressed out cast . . . and crew were working grueling hours to finish . . . on time and under budget, which may have led to the film's most poignant mishap.

The scene called for [Brandon] Lee's character, Eric Draven, to enter his apartment, stumble upon his fiancée's rape, and get shot. (With the major shoot-outs in the can, the firearms consultant had been cut loose.) The

take looked perfect . . . but Brandon didn't get up. The tip of a dummy .44 slug had inadvertently gotten jammed in the barrel of the gun, and the force of the blank sent it into Brandon's abdomen. After five hours of surgery, the 28-year-old actor died. (No criminal charges were filed, and Brandon's mother, Linda Lee Cadwell, settled her negligence suit against the film's producers. The footage of Brandon's death was reportedly destroyed.)

After much deliberation, the filmmakers finished *The Crow* as a tribute to Brandon, and upon its 1994 release, the film grossed more than $50 million domestically. It spawned a TV series and two sequels . . . and cemented a cult following for Brandon much like his father's.

In 1993, Brandon Lee died accidently on the set of The Crow.

know how to regulate the heat. . . . Alas, I produced the spaghetti, permeated with the taste of burned tomatoes. To say the least, it was an unmitigated disaster.[37]

THE CALL

All the time Bruce Lee and his family were in Hong Kong, he kept in close contact with Dozier, hoping to hear news about the *Green Hornet* series. However, it was not until they were back in America, in September of 1965, that he heard anything.

The call from Dozier came through while the Lees were staying in Seattle. The news was good: *The Green Hornet* would begin filming in June of 1966 with Lee as Kato. Bruce Lee had been discovered.

4 Hollywood

In March 1966, Bruce Lee and his family moved to Los Angeles to prepare for his American television debut in *The Green Hornet*. It was an exciting time for the whole family. All of Bruce's and Linda's hard work, sacrifice, and determination was about to pay off. Promised a salary of about four hundred dollars per week, Bruce Lee found the family a small apartment in Westwood, an expensive Los Angeles neighborhood, and began his television career.

THE GREEN HORNET

Based on a 1930s radio serial, *The Green Hornet* was scheduled for thirty half-hour episodes that would follow the adventures of Britt Reid (played by Van Williams), a successful businessman whose secret identity was that of the Green Hornet, a green-clad crime fighter. His sidekick was Kato, played by Bruce Lee. The two masked heroes rode in the Black Beauty, a converted 1966 Chrysler Imperial armed with James Bondesque weapons and devices, tracking down villains and bringing them to justice.

Filming began in June and Lee's perfectionism became immediately apparent. When the director was staging the first fight

scenes, Lee was unhappy. The director was staging the fights in the same way they were typically staged in old Hollywood Westerns, with unconvincing slugging matches. Lee refused to take that approach, determined that his character Kato would fight using

Van Williams (left) and Bruce Lee pose for a Green Hornet *promotional ad.*

Bruce Lee kicks a fictitious villain on The Green Hornet. *Lee was determined to use real kung fu techniques on the show.*

real kung fu. The director agreed under the condition that Lee throw in some flourishes, like high jumping kicks, to please the audiences. Lee consented.

When it came time to film the scenes, there was another problem: Lee was too fast for film; his actions were so lightning quick that they blurred. To solve the problem, Lee had to consciously slow down his actions so that the camera could keep up, something he found difficult to do after so many years of training to increase his speed.

NOT JUST A SIDEKICK

Bruce Lee also had some very specific ideas about how the role of Kato should be played. He was uncomfortable with the racial stereotyping that he saw in American movies and television. Asians were often portrayed as caricatures with pigtails, long wispy beards, and exaggerated buckteeth. They were also portrayed as secretive, crafty, and sinister, or as bumbling laborers or servants. As Linda Lee recalls, "[Bruce Lee] was determined not to lend his talents to that kind of thing."[38]

In a June 1966 letter to Dozier, Lee expressed his concerns that Kato was being written as a mere sidekick. Lee wrote:

> True . . . Kato is a houseboy of Britt [Reid, the Green Hornet], but as the crime fighter, Kato is an "active partner" of the Green Hornet and not a "mute follower."
>
> I . . . feel that at least an occasional dialog would certainly make me "feel" more at home with the fellow players. . . . I feel

that an "active partnership" with the Green Hornet will definitely bring out a more effective and efficient Kato. My aim is for the betterment of the show and I bother you with this only because you [have] been most understanding.[39]

Dozier agreed with Lee. Ultimately, Kato's part was fleshed out to include more dialogue and to establish the character as a more active part of the crime-fighting duo.

CANCELLED

When *The Green Hornet* premiered in September 1966, it was the first time Western audiences had seen kung fu on television. Audiences were amazed, and Lee's fan mail poured in. He was suddenly famous. Linda Lee remembers the pleasure Bruce Lee took in being a celebrity:

> Bruce, like other colorful, bigger-than-life personalities, was delighted by the fame and adulation. . . . He basked in the sunshine of personal appearances, and he even rode on processional floats dressed in the black suit, chauffeur's cap and black mask of his Kato role. He enjoyed it all, and yet, was aware that such publicity was only superficially rewarding. His real reward was in providing quality performances. All other benefits, even financial gain, were only icing on the cake.[40]

Despite the fan mail and positive response, *The Green Hornet* was cancelled after only twenty-six episodes due to poor ratings. Unlike *Batman,* which was played as a campy comedy-action series, *The Green Hornet* was written as a straight action show. Although it was popular with children, the show did not appeal to adults, who felt that the characters were too unbelievable.

MONEY TROUBLES

Even during the filming of *The Green Hornet,* Lee continued training and studying kung fu. On February 5, 1967, he opened a third Jun Fan Gung Fu Institute in Los Angeles. Desiring only serious, sincere students, he did not publicize the school but found students by word of mouth and by recruiting at the National Karate Championship in Washington, D.C.

As with his other schools, it was not money but spreading knowledge of kung fu that had been Lee's motive for opening the school, and the school was not very profitable. With the school as his sole income after the salary from *The Green Hornet* ran out, Lee did not have enough money to pay the bills.

To save money, Lee moved his family to another apartment, working out a deal with the manager to pay a lower rent in exchange for *wing chun* lessons. This arrangement was short-lived, however, because the manager

Lee crouches next to a police car on the set of The Green Hornet. *Despite a positive response from fans, the program was cancelled after only twenty-six episodes.*

had many other such deals with tenants, and the building's owners fired him. Thus, the Lees had to move again into another apartment.

Disappointed with his situation, Lee felt as though he'd taken a step backward in his career, returning to being a kung fu teacher after having glimpsed being an American celebrity. However, one of Lee's friends, Charles FitzSimons, convinced him that he could make a good living teaching private kung fu lessons, particularly if he catered to celebrities.

The idea worked well. Jay Sebring, the Hollywood hair-salon owner who had recommended Lee to Dozier, introduced Lee to celebrities like Lee Marvin, Kareem Abdul-Jabbar, Steve McQueen, James Coburn, and screenwriter Stirling Silliphant. These men became some of Lee's first celebrity clients. On FitzSimons's recommendation, Lee charged them up to $250 an hour for lessons.

Meanwhile, some of the greatest men in martial arts came to Lee for private instruction: Chuck Norris, Joe Lewis, and Mike Stone among them. Lewis, who had first met Lee at the 1967 National Karate Championship in Washington, D.C., recalls his impression of Lee: "In person, Bruce had a charm that didn't come across on the screen. . . . He could just inspire you to love martial arts. . . . He was an incredibly encouraging, inspiring spark of energy."[41]

Chuck Norris, (right), kicks a masked opponent. Norris was one of Lee's first celebrity martial arts clients.

BRUCE LEE ON THE SET

Bruce Lee continued to inspire his students and to develop friendships with many of them, including some of the most famous people in Hollywood at the time. He became particularly good friends with James Coburn, Steve McQueen, and Stirling Silliphant, and these men tried to help Lee succeed in his acting career. With their help, he began picking up some small acting jobs, playing bit parts in series like *Ironside*, *Here Come the Brides*, and *Blondie*.

Silliphant in particular became one of Lee's great champions in Hollywood. He helped Lee get a nonacting job as a fight

NOT-SO-TOUGH GUYS

In Bruce Lee: Fighting Spirit, *Bruce Thomas tells the story of when Bruce Lee met singer Vic Damone in Las Vegas.*

Bruce Lee first came to Silliphant's attention through a story that was making the rounds in Hollywood. The story went that Bruce had met the singer Vic Damone in his Las Vegas hotel suite after one of the singer's performances. Damone had an interest in the martial arts but he had insisted that a tough Italian street brawler would always beat a slightly built Oriental. Damone had two huge bodyguards who also had a low opinion of the martial arts and they were enlisted to prove the point. Bruce agreed to be tested. He asked that one guard be placed behind the door of the suite, with the second man about five feet behind him, smoking a cigarette. Bruce explained that when he came through the door, the first man was to try to stop him. The cigarette was there to represent a holstered gun. Bruce told Damone that before the singer could count to five, he would be through the door and would have knocked the cigarette from the second guy's mouth—"disarming" him. Bruce was further giving them the advantage of telling them exactly what he was going to do, forfeiting the element of surprise.

"If I succeed," said Bruce, "will you take this as an acceptable example of the effectiveness of martial arts?" "Sure," came the disdainful replies. . . .

Suddenly there was a loud wrenching noise as the door flew clear off its hinges, taking the first guard with it, as Bruce followed through in one motion and kicked the cigarette out of the second guard's mouth while he was still frozen in place. The singer managed the comment, "Holy sh——!"

Las Vegas singer, Vic Damone, questioned the value of martial arts until Lee demonstrated its advantages.

No Limits

Both in his personal and professional lives, Bruce Lee believed in never giving up and in never becoming complacent. Quoted in Robert Clouse's book, Bruce Lee: The Biography, *Stirling Silliphant describes Bruce Lee's sometimes merciless drive.*

I was running every day. Bruce had me up to three miles a day.... We'd run the three miles in 21 or 22 minutes, just under eight minutes a mile. So this morning he said we're going to go five. I said, "Bruce, I can't go five. I'm a helluva lot older than you are, and I can't do five." He said, "When we get to three, we'll shift gears and it's only two more, and you'll do it." I said, "Okay, hell, I'll go for it." So we get to three, we get into the fourth mile, and I'm okay for three or four minutes, and then I'm really beginning to give out. I'm tired, my heart's pounding, I can't go anymore and so I say to him, "Bruce, if I run anymore I'm liable to have a heart attack and die." He said, "Then die." It made me so mad that I went the full five miles. Afterward I went to the shower and then I wanted to talk to him about it. I said, ya know, why did you say that? He said, "Because you might as well be dead." He said, "Seriously, if you always put limits on what you can do, physical or anything else, it'll spread over into the rest of your life. It'll spread into your work, into your morality, into your entire being. There are no limits. There are plateaus, but you must not stay there, you must go beyond them. If it kills you, it kills you."

coordinator on the film *The Wrecking Crew,* where Lee used his martial arts expertise to choreograph the film's fight scenes. Silliphant also wrote a fight scene into the screenplay for the film *A Walk in the Spring Rain* for Lee to coordinate.

As a fight coordinator, Lee had to earn the respect of those who had not heard of him; he was short and did not look very threatening. Silliphant recalls bringing Lee onto the set of *A Walk in the Spring Rain.*

The two stuntmen on the picture, who were real Hollywood redneck types,

wondered why I brought this little Chinese guy along. They had never heard of Bruce Lee and [asked] who was this guy to teach them how to fight? . . . Their attitude was very wrong, so I took them aside . . . and told them you better not mess with him. . . . [They didn't listen, so] I told them that we'd have to clear this thing up because they'd be working for him and this wasn't going to help my film, so we'd better have a little demonstration. . . .

So I told Bruce about it and he said, "Yah, gotta straighten these guys out.

No problem." They went out to the swimming pool where Bruce had an airbag and chose the biggest guy first and had him stand about three feet from the edge of the pool, brace himself and hold the bag for protection. Bruce said, "What I'm going to do is stand right in front of you and with no warning, no windup, no run, no nothing, I'm going to kick. I'm going to hit the airbag you're holding. . . . I'll lift you from there out in the air and into the swimming pool. . . . [S]o this guy gets into a kind of crouch, the two of them laughing when Bruce zapped him to catapult him nearly to the other side of the pool. He almost missed the water! . . . But the second guy wasn't convinced. He figured he was tougher. . . . So he really gets braced, I mean he's like a linebacker. Bruce kicked and [he] almost [hit the] other side of the pool. He was up in the air and gone. Those two became slaves of Bruce. Bruce loved it. He loved doing things like that.[42]

In August 1968, Silliphant arranged for Lee's biggest role since *The Green Hornet* by

Stirling Silliphant (far right) and actors Anthony Quinn and Ingrid Bergman on the set of A Walk in the Spring Rain. *Silliphant wrote a fight scene in the movie for Lee to coordinate.*

writing a part for him in a film adaptation of *The Little Sister,* one of author Raymond Chandler's Marlowe detective novels. The film was eventually titled *Marlowe* and starred James Garner as detective Philip Marlowe. Lee played Winslow Wong, a kung fu expert and henchman for the main villain. In one of the film's central scenes, Wong destroys Marlowe's office, culminating with a stunning kick high above his head to shatter a light fixture. Although Lee appeared in only a couple of the film's scenes, it was his first appearance in a full-length American feature film.

LIVING ABOVE HIS MEANS

Finances and prospects were beginning to look better for Bruce Lee, and when Linda Lee discovered she was pregnant again, the couple went looking for a house in Los Angeles. They found, though, that although they had enough money to afford a thirty-thousand-dollar house, this amount was not enough to buy the type of home Bruce Lee wanted. After spending time amongst wealthy Hollywood celebrities, Bruce Lee had seen their houses and cars and wanted the same for himself and his family. The

Lee kicks a light fixture high above his head in a central scene from Marlowe.

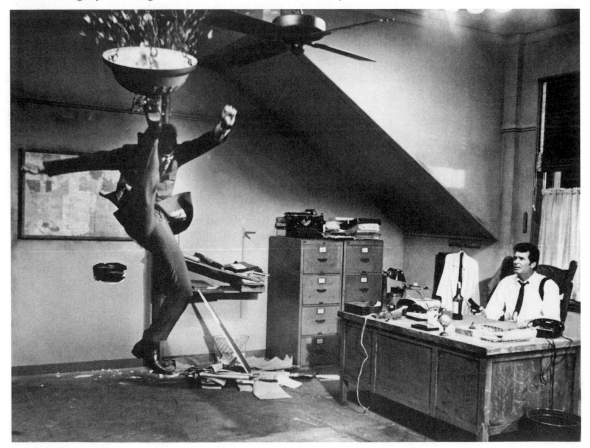

Lees eventually bought a small bungalow in Bel Air for nearly fifty thousand dollars, and soon after they moved in they had problems paying the mortgage.

Despite the money worries, Bruce and Linda Lee were enjoying their new life in Hollywood. Linda Lee writes:

> When I look back on my life with Bruce, it was the years before he became a major star that were the happiest for both of us. Struggling, hoping, wishing, and working for the common goals created a strong bond between us. I am sure this is the way it is with many couples.[43]

HARD TIMES

In 1969, Bruce and Linda Lee's second child, Shannon Lee, was born. The event was happy, but Bruce Lee now had a wife and *two* children to support, an enormous mortgage, and dwindling opportunities in Hollywood. The roles for Asian American actors were few, and those that did exist were usually very small parts that paid little money.

To add to the family's problems, one morning in 1970 Lee injured himself while performing his usual morning exercises. The injury proved serious and caused emotional and financial stress for the family. Linda Lee recalls:

> On this particular day, for whatever reason, Bruce failed to warm up properly before beginning his weightlifting routine. He began by doing what is called a "Good Morning" exercise. Placing a 125-pound barbell across his shoulders, he bent over at the waist and then

Linda Lee and daughter Shannon pose for a photographer.

straightened up. At the time, he felt just a mild twinge of pain in his lower back. In the next few days the pain became severe, causing him to use heat and massage and then eventually seek out a doctor. Over the next few weeks, he underwent extensive examinations. The final diagnosis was that he had injured his fourth sacral nerve, permanently. The doctors advised him to rest in bed and no working out. They told him to forget kung fu, that he would never kick again. Instantly, a black cloud of depression settled over him. Bruce

During a warm-up session, Bruce Lee hurt his back, an injury that prevented him from practicing martial arts for several months.

stayed in bed flat on his back for three months and after that another three months of just moving around the house. . . . I'm sure one can imagine what a desperate time this was for us.[44]

So severely injured that he was unable to teach, act, or do anything to make a living for himself and his family, Lee grew despondent. Desperate and ashamed, he agreed to Linda taking a job.

Bruce Lee was very old-fashioned about the role of women in marriage. Traditionally, Chinese men work and women keep house and raise the children. Bruce felt that Linda's working meant he was an inadequate provider and thus an inadequate man.

Because Bruce was so ashamed that Linda had to work, the Lees conspired to keep her job a secret. She found work in the evenings at a telephone answering service. She took care of Bruce and the kids during the day and then worked at night. When people called in the evening to speak to Linda, Bruce came up with excuses for why she was not at home—he said she was out shopping or at a friend's house. That way, no one ever knew she had a job.

JEET KUNE DO

To make use of his inactive time at home, Lee read voraciously and began writing down ideas and philosophies for a martial arts style he had been developing over the last several years. Ever since the showdown with Wong Jack Man in Oakland, Lee had been reevaluating everything he knew about fighting. The fight had shaken his confidence in his martial arts practice because he had been unable to defeat Wong more quickly and effectively. He came to believe that most martial arts were inadequate for real-life situations. To use traditional methods in a real fight, he thought, was like trying to swim on dry land.

Over the years, Lee researched various martial arts styles and techniques. He attended tournaments to watch other fighters and went to numerous boxing matches. He also studied films of boxing matches, including those of champions like Muhammad Ali and Joe Frazier, slowing the film speed so that he could more closely observe movements and techniques. From his observations and study, he developed

---

WHAT IS *JEET KUNE DO*?

In a 1971 essay entitled "Toward Personal Liberation (Jeet Kune Do)," published in Bruce Lee: Words of the Dragon *(edited by John Little), Bruce Lee describes the philosophy behind* jeet kune do, *the martial art he established in the late 1960s.*

To set the record straight, I have NOT invented a new style, composite, modified, or otherwise, that is a style or method set within distinct form and laws apart from "this" style or "that" method. On the contrary, I hope to free my followers from clinging to styles, patterns, or molds. . . . [J]eet kune do is merely a name used, a mirror in which we see ourselves. The brand name is really nothing special.

Unlike the traditional approach, there is not a series of rules, a classification of techniques, and so forth, that constitute a so-called JKD method of fighting. . . . To create such a method is pretty much like putting a pound of water into wrapping paper and shaping it—although [many] futile arguments exist nowadays as to the choice of colors, textures, and so forth, of the wrapping paper. Briefly, JKD is not a form of specialized conditioning with a set of beliefs and a particular approach. So basically it is not a "mass" art. . . . Consequently, its techniques cannot be reduced to a system. And although it utilizes all ways and means to serve its end . . . it is bound by none and is therefore free from all ways and means.

an all-inclusive style of fighting called *jeet kune do*, "way of the intercepting fist."

The main principle behind *jeet kune do* is that in order to win, a fighter must be able to adapt to any kind of fight and any kind of martial art his opponent uses. The art is called "intercepting fist" because, instead of merely blocking an opponent's attack or punch, one intercepts it and turns it back against the opponent, essentially blocking and attacking at the same time. In 1969, Lee wrote in a letter to William Cheung, his childhood friend from Yip Man's school:

> William, I've lost faith in the Chinese classical arts—though I still call mine Chinese—because basically all styles are products of land swimming, even the Wing Chun school. So my line of training is more toward efficient street fighting with everything goes. . . . I've

named my style jeet kune do. . . . My reason for not sticking to Wing Chun [is] because I sincerely feel that this style has more to offer regarding efficiency.[45]

BACK IN ACTION

After months of remaining sedentary in recovery from his injury, Lee could not bear being still any longer. Being cooped up, unable to practice martial arts or go after his goals, was intolerable, and it pained him that Linda was both having to take care of the children and work. His back problems and pain would last the rest of his life, but he was determined that they not derail his plans for the future. So, against his doctors' advice, he began training and teaching again.

5 Breaking Through

In early 1971, Bruce Lee forced himself to get back to making a living in spite of the pain in his back. Linda Lee's job and the small residuals from *The Green Hornet* were inadequate to support the family of four in their Bel Air home. As a result, Bruce Lee began teaching kung fu again, and he tried to get his career in Hollywood on track.

Lee's highest ambition was to make kung fu known throughout the world, and he knew that television and film were the way to make that happen. But, beyond the odd jobs that Silliphant and others found or created for him, Lee worried that in Hollywood he would never be able to get the kind of acting work he wanted. Writes Bruce Thomas:

> Nobody knew quite what to do with him. More to the point, nobody was willing to risk money on an unknown actor who also happened to be Chinese. It must have made Bruce question more than once the time he had spent fighting his fellow countrymen for the right to teach kung fu to Westerners.[46]

"TOO CHINESE" FOR *KUNG FU*

Bruce Lee suffered a big disappointment during the early 1970s. He had been work-ing with Warner Brothers television executives on an idea for a television pilot about the adventures of a Shaolin warrior-priest who used kung fu against outlaws in the American Old West. Lee was closely involved with the project from the beginning and hoped to return to television as the lead in the series. Lee saw this new project, which had the working title *The Warrior*, as a good opportunity to further his goals of spreading the art of kung fu because so much of the plot depended on martial arts.

However, when the National Broadcasting Company (NBC) decided to produce the pilot, they gave the lead role to a Caucasian actor, David Carradine. Network executives said Lee looked "too Chinese" for the lead role of Caine, a former Shaolin monk. They worried that audiences would not accept an Asian in the lead role. Robert Clouse writes:

> Bruce Lee was devastated. Here was a script with a Chinese background, with a Chinese in the lead role and based on the Chinese culture, and they gave it to a [white man]. The network . . . and various sponsors felt a Chinese could not carry the lead role on American television.[47]

David Carradine as Caine in the television series Kung Fu. *Network executives chose Carradine for the role because they thought Bruce Lee looked "too Chinese."*

It was clear that the network executives chose David Carradine because he was white. No more famous than Bruce Lee at the time, Carradine had no martial arts experience at all. The pilot was retitled *Kung Fu* and went on to become a highly popular series, making David Carradine famous.

THE KING OF HONG KONG

In the spring of 1970, to give himself a break from his troubles in the United States, Bruce Lee took his son Brandon to Hong Kong; Linda and Shannon stayed behind in Los Angeles. The trip was also planned so that he could arrange for Grace Lee to come live in America. Grace was still mourning the loss of her husband, Hoi Chuen, and Bruce Lee wanted her to live closer to him so that he could take care of her.

When he got on the plane in Los Angeles, Lee had no idea of the reception that would be waiting for him when he landed. After its cancellation in the United States, syndicated episodes of *The Green Hornet* had been broadcast throughout Hong Kong. Translated into Mandarin, the series—called *The Kato Show* in the East, had made Bruce Lee very famous in Hong Kong. Since he lived in America, though, Lee had no idea of his fame.

When he got off the plane, hundreds of people were waiting for him. Linda Lee writes:

> He returned to find every Chinese breast swollen with pride at the achievement of the hometown boy in America. Newspapers demanded interviews, radiomen stuck microphones in front of his face and he was invited to appear on Hong Kong's two TV channels. The old films he had made as a child star were now among the most popular offerings on these channels.[48]

Lee happily obliged with interviews and appearances. He put on kung fu demonstrations for Hong Kong television and even brought five-year-old Brandon with him on some appearances to show off his son's growing prowess in martial arts.

RUN RUN SHAW'S OFFER

While in Hong Kong, Bruce Lee decided to look into getting involved in the movie business there. Although he knew that the movie business in Hong Kong was greatly different than it was in Hollywood, he was frustrated with the lack of opportunity in Hollywood and had a friend contact Run Run Shaw, the cofounder of the largest

David Carradine's role on Kung Fu *made him famous.*

movie studio in Hong Kong. At that time Shaw was paying actors at his studios approximately forty dollars a month. Actors lived at the studio in cheap concrete dormitories and worked under poor conditions with old or malfunctioning equipment, inadequate direction, and frequently no scripts. Still, Lee thought it was worth finding out what opportunity his Hong Kong fame would provide him. He had already been an actor in Hong Kong and thought that his American fame from *The Green Hornet* and *Marlowe* might give him more clout than the average Hong Kong actors had. Lee made a proposal to Shaw to do a film for ten thousand dollars.

Even though Shaw was aware of Lee's popularity, the proposal seemed absurd. Shaw himself was extraordinarily wealthy; Lee biographer Tom Bleecker quotes estimates of the Shaw family fortune at being worth between $200 million to $1 billion. But Shaw believed actors, directors, and technicians were interchangeable and not very important. It was unprecedented for an actor to request such a salary. Shaw answered the proposal with an offer for Lee to act in an upcoming film for seventy-five dollars a week. Lee would also be contracted to the company for seven years, with the potential of one day earning up to two hundred dollars a week.

Lee did not even bother to respond. He got on a plane and returned home.

The Silent Flute

Despite his popularity in Hong Kong, the disappointment over losing the role in

Kung Fu was hard on Lee. Still, he was determined to continue pursuing a film career in America. He believed that Hollywood was still the best means for achieving his goals. Tired of waiting for projects to come to him, he decided to develop a film for himself.

During the late 1960s, Lee had a recurring dream that he used as the inspiration for a film concept. The dream was about a character searching for answers to many of the enduring philosophical questions Lee had, such as the purpose of life. But even though the character's quest resembled his own, Lee decided not to try to write the lead role for himself, believing that the film would have a better chance for success if the lead character were white. Instead, Lee would appear as various animals and as the main character's spiritual guide. Bruce Thomas writes:

> It was a "hero's quest" story, tracing a martial artist's evolution towards self-understanding. On the way there would be trials and revelations, battles with others, and battles with his own doubts and fears. . . . He decided to play several supporting roles, as animals and elemental characters that the hero would have to overcome on his journey. Bruce would also appear at times as the hero's guide.[49]

Lee asked his student and friend, actor Steve McQueen, to play the role of Cord. At that time McQueen was at the height of his fame, having finished *The Thomas Crown Affair*, one of his most successful films, in 1968. But McQueen was not interested in *The Silent Flute* because he thought the film was

A New Trend

In his pursuit of quality in his martial arts and acting, Bruce Lee set an example that would change the way the Hong Kong film industry operated. In a 1971 interview with The Hong Kong Star, *published in* Bruce Lee: Words of the Dragon *(edited by John Little), Lee spoke about his ambition to change the way films are made in the East and West.*

What I am trying to do is start a whole trend of martial art films in the U.S. To me, they are much more interesting than the gun-slinging sagas of the West. In the Westerns you are dealing solely with guns. Here, we deal with everything. [Martial art] is an expression of the human body. [As for Chinese action films,] you have to be careful of movies that have broadly an action kick. It does not matter, it seems, whether a Chinese movie has a central theme as long as there are so many feet of action. I don't go for that and I have achieved mutual cooperation with [the Hong Kong film studio] Golden Harvest in the sense we are going with . . . the main theme in mind.

Lee performs a flying kick. His ideas about filmmaking revolutionized the way martial arts films were produced.

Actor Steve McQueen refused to co-star with Lee on The Silent Flute.

designed primarily to make Lee famous. McQueen told his friend:

> Let's face it, Bruce, this is a vehicle to make a big star out of you, and I gotta be honest with you, I'm not in this business to make stars out of other people. I love you, buddy, but you're just going to be hanging on my coattails, and I'm just not going to do that. I'm not going to carry you on my back.[50]

Lee was an intensely proud man, and this rebuff wounded and angered him. After this rebuff, he was determined to become a bigger star than McQueen one day.

Lee found other friends to be more interested, at least initially. When he presented

the idea to James Coburn and Stirling Silliphant, they agreed to help with the project. Coburn signed on to play the lead role and Silliphant pledged to help develop the story and find someone to write the script. The men met for two hours three times a week for three months, and soon each of them was excited about the project. The script went through several difficult drafts and various writers. Finally Lee, Coburn, and Silliphant wrote it themselves. The combination of Coburn and Silliphant's show-business insights and Lee's martial arts knowledge produced what they believed was a unique script that had the potential to launch Lee's film career and also provide movie audiences with the first authentic American martial arts film.

DIFFICULT TIMES IN INDIA

Like McQueen, Coburn was at the height of his fame in the 1960s and 1970s. Because Coburn was involved with the project, Warner Brothers, one of the biggest Hollywood studios, agreed to produce *The Silent Flute*. However the studio added a condition—one that would prove damaging to the potential film. Because Warner Brothers had money invested in Indian film-production companies, the studio required that *The Silent Flute* be filmed there. Understanding the difficulty of filming abroad, particularly in an economically underdeveloped country like India, Coburn and Silliphant were reluctant to pursue the film. But Lee was adamant about continuing. He had invested so much of his time and emotional energy in the script that he could not bear to give up. He also worried that an opportunity like this might not come up again. Lee was able to persuade Coburn and Silliphant to change their minds, and in 1971 the three men booked a flight to India to scout locations for the film.

The trip proved to be a difficult one. The three men spent days in a car, driving all over India to find a location in which to shoot the film. Many of the roads were unpaved and dusty, it was hot for most of the trip, and the lack of facilities and accessible roads for film equipment and crews made

Stirling Silliphant initially agreed to help Lee with The Silent Flute.

most of the locations the men found inadequate for filming.

After several days of sitting in a car, bumping along on bad roads, Lee's back injury began to hurt terribly. The pain, along with his frustration at the failure to find a film location, put him in a bad mood. Additionally, egos and tempers began to clash and flare among the men as they grew irritable from the long, fruitless journey. Silliphant recalls:

> [I]n the car, Mr. Coburn always sat in the front seat and Bruce and I sat in the backseat. Bruce had sort of a curious habit of humming pop songs under his breath, mile after mile, which irritated the hell out of Coburn. Coburn finally turned around to Bruce and said, "For Christ's sake will you stop that. You're driving me crazy!" Bruce was crushed. I will never forget when Jimmy turned back, Bruce shook his fist at the back of Jimmy's head and it started the friction between the [two men]. It was that way all through India. The trip was horrible. . . . We were in the car hours and hours together. There would be humor and we would laugh, and then we would sleep, and then we'd talk about the film, and then there would be little anger spurts between the two of them. . . . We were coming apart.[51]

Lee also resented the disparity in the way he and Coburn were treated. Because of Coburn's wealth and fame, he stayed in the most lavish hotel suites while Lee got only small rooms. Lee became frustrated because he felt that, as far as the film project went, he was Coburn's equal.

Additionally, unlike Lee, Coburn and Silliphant were successful in show business and had many projects awaiting them. Lee thought that Coburn's and Silliphant's level of personal investment in the film was less than his own. He felt this was confirmed when, after weeks of searching unsuccessfully for locations, the two decided to quit and go back to America. Silliphant continues:

> The result was when we came back from India he [Lee] was truly in the depths of despair. His two partners, Jimmy and I, were not going to recommend [the film]. . . . Bruce at that time was so desperate to become a star and believed so much in *The Silent Flute* that he felt to hell with the locations, we'll make it work. . . .

> "Let's go guys, let's do it. We've got a hot company, they want to do it, why don't we do it?" [Bruce said]. Jimmy and I said no.[52]

With Coburn off the project, Warner Brothers pulled their finances. Lee was disappointed, but he eventually had to let the project go.

The Silent Flute would not be revived until after Bruce Lee's death. In 1978, David

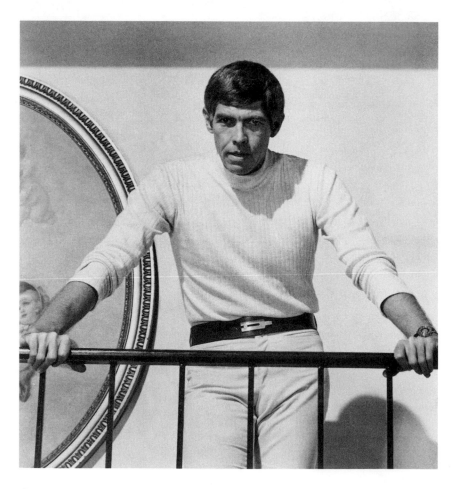

Actor James Coburn ultimately chose not to participate in The Silent Flute.

David Carradine plays a blind flute player in Circle of Iron, *an adapted version of Lee's* The Silent Flute.

Carradine bought the rights to *The Silent Flute*. Although Bruce Lee's name was used in the credits numerous times, the film, retitled *Circle of Iron*, bears little resemblance to the original concept or script.

ADVERSITY

The losses of *Kung Fu* and *The Silent Flute* were significant disappointments to Lee, yet he refused to admit defeat. He believed that adversity was not only an inescapable part of life but that it also made him stronger and

provided him with a better understanding of the world and himself. He wrote:

> Never waste energy on worries and negative thoughts. I mean, who has the most insecure job as I have? What do I live on? My faith in my ability that I'll make it. Sure my back screwed me up good for a year but with every adversity comes a blessing because a shock acts as a reminder to oneself that we must not get stale in routine. . . . In a time when everything goes well, my mind is pampered with

enjoyment, possessiveness, etc. Only in times of adversity, privation, or mishap, does my mind function and think properly of my state. The close examination of self strengthens my mind and leads me to understand and be understood.[53]

Lee's ability to remain philosophical and positive during difficult times was of great importance to his success. Although he suffered frustration, anger, and sadness, he was always able to turn these emotions around and get back on track. Linda Lee writes: "Above all, he had the saving grace of always being able to laugh at himself. When he was going through a particularly bad period and feeling low, he erected a little sign on his desk, which simply said WALK ON."[54]

LONGSTREET

When Lee had returned from Hong Kong to Los Angeles in 1970, Silliphant wrote a significant part for him into the pilot of a new television series called *Longstreet*. The show starred actor James Franciscus as a blind detective. In the pilot episode entitled "The Way of the Intercepting Fist" (the translation of Lee's martial art *jeet kune do*) Lee played an antiques dealer and martial arts instructor who taught the detective how to fight and defend himself.

Longstreet was a perfect opportunity for Lee to work toward spreading knowledge of kung fu, which had been a goal of his since he moved to the United States. Thus

Lee accepted the part, which many critics agree was one of his best acting performances.

Silliphant wrote the episode using his own experience as a student of Lee's. In one scene, for instance, Lee's character encourages the blind detective to sharpen his nonimpaired senses in an effort to better defend himself. The scene was based on an actual exercise Lee and Silliphant performed; Lee blindfolded Silliphant and taught him to use his other senses to know where his opponent was and how to anticipate an attack without seeing it.

Actor James Franciscus starred in the television series Longstreet.

The authenticity of the script and Lee's appearance made the episode the series' most popular. Silliphant describes the response:

> We had more fan mail on that episode than any other in the series. I like to think that that episode was his first good film—the first to show him off to the world as an Oriental martial artist with pride and dignity. On that first *Longstreet* Bruce was shown as a perfect teacher, the mystic simplicity of his lessons really came through. It is still one of the best martial arts shows I've ever seen on the air.[55]

OFFER FROM ABROAD

During the months following his return from Hong Kong, Lee kept in contact with the Hong Kong media by giving numerous telephone interviews for Hong Kong radio stations and newspapers. His press in Hong Kong was almost unanimously positive, and one of the people who followed these stories with increasing interest was Raymond Chow. Chow owned Golden Harvest Studios in Kowloon, a low-budget competitor to Run Run Shaw's studio.

In 1971, Chow called Lee with an offer: two films for fifteen thousand dollars. Chow also would not require the usual long-term contract that most Hong Kong actors had to sign in order to work.

Lee spent some time considering the offer, deciding whether the money and opportunity were good enough to merit the time away from Hollywood. One of the most appealing factors, though, was that he saw he could improve the quality of Chinese martial arts movies. Linda Lee writes:

> While considering the contract, Bruce spent a great deal of time reviewing the most recent Mandarin movies. As he said later, "They were awful. . . . [W]hat really bothered me was that they all fought exactly the same way. Wow, nobody's really like that. When you get into a fight, everybody reacts differently, and it is possible to act and fight at the same time. Most Chinese films have been very superficial and one-dimensional."[56]

Coburn and Silliphant told Lee to demand more money, but Lee, tired of waiting, did not want to miss the opportunity. Further, he did not know how long it would be before Hollywood made him an offer equal to this. After taking all of these factors into account, he accepted Chow's offer.

HONOR

Within days of accepting Chow's offer, he got another offer from another studio, this one in Thailand, for more money. Lee said, "The guy told me to rip up the contract [with Chow] and he'd top Raymond [Chow]'s offer and even take care of any lawsuit for breaking the agreement."[57] Although the larger salary was appealing, Lee did not think it was honorable to break a contract. He declined.

BRUCE LEE ON VIOLENCE

In a 1971 interview with the Hong Kong newspaper The China Mail, *published in* Bruce Lee: Words of the Dragon *(edited by John Little), Bruce Lee discusses the issue of violence in his kung fu films and in martial arts in general.*

I have to make one point clear. That is, a movie is not made by Bruce Lee alone and one can never dictate the quality of a film. It is the product produced first by the script-writer, then the director, actors, and a lot of working members. So, if I make a movie that is a bad influence on its audience, I should not bear the whole responsibility. Nevertheless, I still have the following wishes: One, I never want to make a movie for the sake of cruelty. I will first examine the reasons why the characters have to fight. Are these reasons sufficient? If not, I will not join in. Two, because martial art is my career, I want to use it as a means to express my ideals. A real fighter should fight for righteousness. Moreover, when he decides to fight, he must be sincere and fight wholeheartedly to the end. Only in such a way can he develop good character and total truth and sincerity. Like the way I am talking now, I am being totally sincere and am prepared to tell you all that I know. And I am trying

my best to answer your questions. If everyone does a thing wholeheartedly and sincerely for their ideals, then money will become a secondary question. However, I can see that in filmmaking, not many people have principles to follow. Most are speculators, they do everything for money. They propagandize violence and cruelty for no reason in their films.

Bruce Lee had specific ideas about the use of violence in films.

In July 1971, Lee boarded a flight to Bangkok, Thailand; the first Chow film would be shot in the little village of Pak Chong, just north of Bangkok. When Lee exited the plane, Chow met him at the airport.

It was the first time the two men had met in person, and they took an instant liking to each other. Lee's first words to Chow were "You just wait, I'm going to be the biggest Chinese star in the world."[58]

6 King of Hong Kong

Although the fifteen thousand dollars Lee would be paid to make two films with Chow's Golden Harvest Studios was not much money by Hollywood standards, it was a huge paycheck for an actor in the East. By U.S. standards, the budget for the first film was low—only one hundred thousand dollars—and working conditions were terrible. The crew used mostly old or broken equipment, and injuries, bad climate, and illness plagued Lee and the rest of the cast. In a letter to his wife dated July 24, 1971, Lee wrote:

> Pakchong is something else. The mosquitoes are terrible and the cockroaches are all over the place. Of course, the main reason for not having written is for lack of services, but also, I had a rather nasty accident—as I was washing a super thin glass, my grip broke and the damn thing cut my right hand rather deep—the worst cut I have, that requires ten stitches. . . .
>
> I'm writing rather poorly due to my hand—it's much better now—I'm taking my vitamin pills and though I'm down to 128 [pounds], I'm getting used to the conditions here—the cockroaches are a constant threat, the lizards I can ignore.[59]

In addition to the cut on his hand, Lee suffered other physical injuries. He sprained his ankle during a stunt, and in some of the film's scenes the director had to film Lee in close-ups only so that his limp from the injury would not be visible. Further, his back injury was so bad that he needed rest and injections of pain medication after every scene.

THE BIG BOSS

Lee's first film for Golden Harvest was called *The Big Boss* (released in the United States as *Fists of Fury*). The plot concerns a Japanese mob boss and his Thai gangsters who terrorize a Chinese community in Bangkok. Lee plays Cheng Chao An, a martial artist who left China for Thailand after getting into trouble with the Chinese police for fighting. In the film's climax, Lee as Cheng defeats twenty Thai gangsters who wield knives, clubs, and chains.

Lee was a perfectionist, and his highest concern was always the quality of whatever project he was involved in. From the start of the film shoot, Lee's patience was tested by what he saw as a lack of professionalism and the poor conditions on the set. The first director assigned to the film had a violent temper and constantly screamed at the cast and crew until he was fired from the film. The second director, Lo Wei, was hardly an improvement over the first. Lee disliked Lo Wei from the start because of the director's lack of attention to the film. Bruce Thomas writes:

> A compulsive gambler, Lo Wei was far more concerned with what was going on at the racetrack than what was happening on the film set. Because sound was not recorded at the same time as the action was filmed, Lo Wei arranged to have the commentary of the horse races booming across the set while the actors were attempting to play a scene.[60]

"LEE THREE LEGS"

Lee worked hard to make *The Big Boss* as good as it could possibly be. In addition to his acting role, he took on the jobs of script doctor and fight coordinator. He particularly excelled as fight coordinator, and his efforts and abilities did not go unnoticed by the people he worked with. Lee's fighting skill made him particularly popular with the stuntmen. Robert Clouse writes:

> Some of the world's finest stuntmen are the Chinese working out of Hong Kong and several were sent to Thailand to work with Bruce on the picture. When

In the climactic battle of The Big Boss, *Lee stands ready to fight the last of twenty Thai gangsters.*

Lee performs a difficult high jump kick. His skill usually impressed the people he worked with.

they returned, they praised this new man to everyone and called him "Lee sum geok," or "Lee three legs." It meant Bruce was so lightning fast it seemed he had three legs. The stuntmen never lost their respect and admiration for Bruce. They were always there to help or protect him.[61]

During the filming of *The Big Boss*, the pilot episode of *Longstreet* opened to excellent reviews. The network sent repeated telegrams to Golden Harvest trying to track down Lee, hoping he would agree to appear in more episodes—at a thousand dollars an episode. When Lee got the offer, he took the risk of asking the network for double the money and got it. He signed a contract to appear in

several more episodes. Lee hoped his goal of American stardom was now possible. All he had to do was complete one more film for Chow and go back to the United States to the television career awaiting him.

THE BIG HIT

With the promise of the money from the *Longstreet* contract and the next Golden Harvest film, Linda Lee was able to quit her job at the telephone answering service. She was also able to fly with Bruce and their children to Hong Kong to attend the premiere of *The Big Boss*. She recalls their arrival in Hong Kong:

I'll never forget our arrival at the Hong Kong airport. Bruce had told me that there would probably be some people meeting us at the airport, so as we approached our landing in Hong Kong I changed my clothes and prepared to meet whomever was there to greet us. Nothing could have prepared me, however, for the masses of fans and reporters that applauded Bruce's return. A group of Boy Scouts held up a banner to greet us, flashbulbs were going off everywhere, and the crowds of people threatened to become a security problem for the airport police. It was my first exposure to what it was going to be like to be the wife of a movie star, and it filled me with pride as well as some trepidation about how our lives were changing and this was before *The Big Boss* had even premiered.[62]

The night of the premiere, Bruce Lee was nervous about the response to the film. Hong Kong audiences are notorious for being vocal and even violent about their displeasure over a movie they disliked; some have even resorted to cutting up theater seats with knives. When the lights came up after the end of *The Big Boss*, though, there was a long moment of uncertain silence, and then the audience cheered. The film was a success. Robert Clouse describes the overall response:

> [With *The Big Boss*] the Chinese started a life-long love affair with Bruce that failed to abate with his death. He did more for the Chinese psyche than any dozen politicians and martyrs. [The film] acted as gut-level therapy for millions of overworked and underprivileged people. . . . Bruce rekindled a feeling of pride and literally brought his countrymen to their feet screaming and cheering in hundreds of theaters.[63]

The Big Boss broke box-office records in Hong Kong. In less than three weeks, the film grossed more than HK $3.5 million in

A STAR IS BORN

Bruce Lee's first major martial arts feature film was The Big Boss *(released in the United States as* Fists of Fury*). In her biography,* The Bruce Lee Story, *Linda Lee recalls the night the film premiered in Hong Kong.*

That night every dream that Bruce had ever had came true as the audience rose to its feet with thunderous, cheering applause. In less than two hours of action on the screen, Bruce became a glittering star, and as we left the theater we were absolutely mobbed. One American entertainment critic wrote, "that film is the finest action job of Bruce Lee's career. It is one of the most outstanding examples of sheer animal presence on [film] ever produced. I would match it against the best of Clint Eastwood, Steve McQueen or the various James Bonds."

Hong Kong alone, more than a million dollars higher than the proceeds from the prior record holder, *The Sound of Music.* As James Coburn remarked, Bruce Lee was suddenly the Golden Boy, the King of Hong Kong.

THE BATTLE OVER BRUCE LEE

During the filming of *The Big Boss,* Chow came to meet Lee on the set to work out the details for the second film, which would be called *Fist of Fury* (released in the United States as *The Chinese Connection*). This was only the second time the two men had met, but they got along well. However, it became clear that their professional goals for the future differed. Chow recognized the prize he had in his new star and wanted to convince Lee to stay with Golden Harvest. Lee, on the other hand, saw his future in America and was eager to finish his contractual obligation to Chow and get back to the United States to take advantage of television offers there.

Taking note of Lee's celebrity and fame, Run Run Shaw also tried to entice Lee to stay in Hong Kong, although Shaw wanted

Lee in a scene from Fist of Fury, *his second film for Golden Harvest studios.*

THE THIRTEENTH FLOOR

In The Bruce Lee Story, *Linda Lee recalls the Hong Kong apartment where she and Bruce Lee lived with their children during the filming of* Fist of Fury *in 1971.*

It was a small place with two bedrooms, a living room and dining room, and a Chinese kitchen. A lot of modern conveniences that I had been used to, such as a washer and dryer were missing. Our clothes were washed by hand and hung out the window on bamboo poles to dry. The windows had bars on them for security reasons as do most houses in Hong Kong, even though our flat was on the 13th floor. The building was equipped with elevators, but they frequently broke down and we would all have to trudge up and down the 13 floors. Actually, it got to be sort of fun, so Bruce and I used to run up and down the stairs for exercise. Our neighbors thought we were a bit strange.

to steal him away from Golden Harvest even before the next film could be made. Shaw sent Lee a check for $248,000 and a signed contract. Lee turned the deal down, however, remaining faithful to his commitment to Chow. Shaw tried again later, this time sending a blank check while filming was under way on the second Golden Harvest film, but again Lee declined.

FIST OF FURY

During the filming of *Fist of Fury*, Bruce and Linda Lee sold their Bel Air home and settled in Hong Kong, enrolling Brandon Lee in La Salle College, the same school that Bruce had been expelled from fourteen years earlier. Chow, trying to keep his star happy, went to some modest expense to make Lee and his family at home in Hong Kong. He provided the family with an apartment in Kowloon, close to where Lee had grown up. The Lees settled in for the duration of the film.

Lee began work on *Fist of Fury* in early 1972. The lack of professionalism he had endured on the set of *The Big Boss* in Thailand was also a problem in the Golden Harvest studios in Hong Kong. Director Lo Wei was called in again, as were many of the same cast members.

Lo Wei and Lee had numerous disagreements over the film. Both men were quick-tempered, stubborn, and had very different ideas about filmmaking. Thus, they frequently fought for control over the direction of the film. Lee's perfectionism clashed with Lo Wei's working style. The director wanted to get the film shot quickly, while Lee wanted it shot well, even if it required numerous takes of scenes.

Lee kicks a Japanese man's head in Fist of Fury. *His character's defeat of the film's Japanese villains thrilled moviegoers in Hong Kong.*

NATIONAL HERO

In spite of the troubles during the filming of *Fist of Fury,* the film proved to be another huge success. Set in Shanghai at the turn of the twentieth century, the film follows the story of a Chinese martial artist who tracks down the Japanese men who murdered his instructor. The plot called up memories of the atrocities that occurred to Hong Kong Chinese during the Japanese occupation in World War II, and drew upon the long-standing history of animosity between the two groups. The film set Lee up to be the defender and champion of the Chinese so that when Lee's character triumphed, Chinese audiences were symbolically victorious.

In one of the film's central scenes, Lee single-handedly defeats an entire school of Japanese karate practitioners. In response to this and other scenes like it in the film, many viewers in Hong Kong climbed on top of their theater seats, applauding and cheering. Bruce Thomas writes that the film's nationalistic appeal changed Lee's status as a public figure:

> *Fist of Fury* dug deep into the Chinese popular feelings. The Chinese had been plundered and exploited for centuries by stronger powers. For hundreds of years the relationship between the Chinese and Japanese was one of open hostility, punctuated by regular periods of war. . . . Bruce was well aware of national feelings and played shamelessly on them. . . . By the end of [the film], Bruce Lee had advanced from being a supreme screen fighter who was genuinely as good as he appeared to becom-

ing much more. He had done something dreamed of by every politician: he was now a household name. He had become a national hero.[64]

THE DISCOMFORTS OF FAME

The success of *Fist of Fury* ultimately surpassed even that of *The Big Boss*. On its opening night in Hong Kong, thousands of fans rushed the theater, causing a traffic jam that lasted for hours. Crowds lined up to see the film, and scalpers sold tickets in the streets for as much as eighteen times their face value. In the Philippines, the film ran for more than six months. In Hong Kong, theaters stopped showing *Fist of Fury* for weeks to give other films a chance to make some money.

Bruce Lee was the best known man in Hong Kong, but the celebrity status that he had so often hoped for was not easy to live with. As his mother Grace had told him when he was a boy, the life of a film star was not as comfortable as he had thought. He could not walk through the streets without crowds of fans blocking his way. He could not go out for a meal without soon being surrounded by patrons and waiters clamoring for autographs. Film producers from studios all over Asia were so desperate to get him to work for them that many gave him checks for large sums of money without telling him what the money was for, hoping to trick him into a legal commitment to work for them if he cashed the checks. Producers even enlisted acquaintances of Lee's to help them. Eventually, Lee did not know whom he could trust. In a 1972 interview with *Black*

Lee was skeptical of stardom and fame.

Belt magazine, Bruce Lee spoke about the discomforts of fame:

> I had a heck of a problem. I had people stop by my door and just pass me a check for $200,000. When I asked them what it was for they replied, "Don't worry, it's just a gift for you." I mean, I didn't even know these people. When people pass out big money—just like that—you don't know what to think. I destroyed all the checks but it was difficult to do because I didn't know what they were for. Sure, money is important

As a film star, Lee had to deal with corrupt friends and producers.

in providing for my family, but it isn't everything. I didn't know who to trust and I even grew suspicious of my old pals. I was in a period when I didn't know who was trying to take advantage of me.[65]

THE WAY OF THE DRAGON

Having fulfilled his contract with Golden Harvest, Bruce Lee was now free to pursue other offers. He returned to the United States in 1972 to what he believed would be a thriving television career. As it turned out, though, the *Longstreet* episodes for which he had signed a contract were mostly walk-on appearances that did not give him much opportunity to act or demonstrate his kung fu to audiences.

Additionally, even though his financial problems had been eliminated and his popularity had risen, Lee remained disappointed by the lack of significant roles available for him in American movies. Frustrated, he again looked to Hong Kong.

Lee was determined not to go back to work for Golden Harvest. His creative differences with Lo Wei and his personal ambitions made it difficult for him to continue working for a studio where he could not be in control. Lee wanted complete control over his next film. So instead of simply signing a new contract, he approached Chow, suggesting that they become partners in a new production company. Chow, mindful of Lee's popularity, agreed. The partnership resulted in a production company called Concord, and the first film Lee and Chow produced

LOSING FRIENDS

In his book, Bruce Lee: Fighting Spirit, *Bruce Thomas describes how fame ended one of Lee's close friendships in the fall of 1972.*

When Bruce had returned to Hong Kong in 1970, his childhood friend Unicorn had acted as a go-between when Bruce was sounding out a possible deal to make a film with Shaw Brothers. Now Unicorn asked Bruce if he would return the favor and help him with the fight choreography on a film he was making on a shoestring budget, to be called *The Unicorn Palm.*

Bruce always tried to help his friends. He had already given Unicorn the role of head waiter in *Way of the Dragon* and now he agreed to help his friend again. . . . Filming started in 1972. It soon became obvious that Unicorn was out of his depth as a leading actor and again Bruce had to back his friend. As well as supervising the fight action, Bruce came up with several script ideas, spending a day at the set while the cameras rolled.

When the film was released soon afterwards, Bruce Lee's name was given star billing and he was credited not only as the martial arts advisor but as a leading actor. Footage of Bruce arriving on the set and of him rehearsing the actors had been contrived to fit into a new storyline. Bruce could only issue a legal letter condemning the sorry project. . . . [H]e was angered and saddened by the incident which had both betrayed his trust and increased his feelings of suspicion.

was *The Way of the Dragon* (released in the United States as *Return of the Dragon*), based on a script that Lee wrote himself.

LABOR OF LOVE

The Way of the Dragon was a labor of love for Lee. He began work on the project in early 1972, learning as much as possible about filmmaking by buying and reading dozens of books dealing with everything from directing to set building. He intended to make the film almost entirely by himself so that he could retain complete control over its quality.

Based on Lee's own early experiences as a waiter at Ruby Chow's, the plot concerns Tang Lung (China Dragon), a young man from the Chinese countryside who goes to Rome on vacation. There he meets a woman who owns a restaurant that is under threat of being taken over by mobsters. Tang helps the woman keep her business by teaching all the waiters at the restaurant how to use kung fu

In the climactic scene from The Way of the Dragon, *Lee (right) battles the villain, played by Chuck Norris.*

and dueling with the arch villain (played by Lee's student and friend Chuck Norris) in a climactic scene at the Colosseum.

Lee did not anticipate how time-consuming and difficult work on *The Way of the Dragon* would be. He did not have the required permits to film in many of the European locations required for the movie. Further, he and his film crew did not speak the local languages, making location shots difficult. The postproduction work on the film, such as editing, dubbing the soundtrack (most films in Asia record the dialogue after the film is shot because it is cheaper and easier), and adding the musical

score also proved more complicated than Lee had anticipated.

The film took an enormous amount of time and energy from Lee, and he insisted that everyone on the project work with equal commitment. Linda Lee writes:

> Undoubtedly there were some who felt that Bruce was difficult to work with in that he constantly demanded perfection in himself and everyone around him, but he knew what he wanted and how to get it. Admittedly, he was very blunt and outspoken when he felt it necessary, but all things considered, he kept

himself on a totally professional level throughout the entire production.[66]

Lee's hard work was rewarded when *The Way of the Dragon* was released in late 1972. As with his last two films, it broke box-office records, earning HK $5 million.

THE GAME OF DEATH

Even though Lee continued to hope that his career in the United States would improve, his success in Hong Kong was undeniable. Thus, Lee began another project with Chow and their Concord production company. The film would be called *The Game of Death.*

Although Lee had not yet worked out a script for the film, the concept involved a main character (played by Lee) who had to penetrate a pagoda (a tower made up of several stories) to kill the main villain. Each story would be guarded by a master of a different martial art whom Lee's character would have to defeat to get to the villain, who waited on the top level.

Lee believed this concept would allow him to demonstrate the superiority of *jeet kune do*. The philosophy of *jeet kune do* is that a fighter must not rely on any one martial art or style; rather, to be successful, a fighter must be able to adapt to whatever the situation calls for. In the film, Lee's character would defeat masters of various martial arts

Lee fights off an intruder in The Way of the Dragon. *The film broke box-office records.*

because he could adapt, while they were constrained by their classical styles.

In late 1972, Lee began preliminary work on the film. One of the first tasks was casting. He planned to cast the most talented array of martial artists available, including his friends Dan Inosanto and Chuck Norris. These men would play the guards of the pagoda. Lee decided that the main villain, the giant, would be played by his student, basketball star Kareem Abdul-Jabbar.

Abdul-Jabbar was cast early, and Lee began shooting some of the fight scenes with him before the script was begun. Abdul-Jabbar's height exceeded seven feet; Lee was nearly two feet shorter. Lee wanted to use this difference in stature to demonstrate that he could fight anyone of any size.

AMERICA CALLS

With Lee's new project under way, numerous offers continued to arrive. The popularity of *The Big Boss* and *Fist of Fury* spread beyond Asia and to the United States. Soon

In The Game of Death, *Lee fights Kareem Abdul-Jabbar. Lee chose Abdul-Jabbar as the film's villain to demonstrate that he could defeat anyone of any size using* jeet kune do.

CHALLENGING THE MASTER

As a preeminent practitioner of kung fu and a growing celebrity, Bruce Lee faced continual challenges from young men who wanted to try their own martial arts skill on him. This March 1973 article in the Hong Kong newspaper The China Mail, *published in* Bruce Lee: Words of the Dragon *(edited by John Little), details one widely publicized incident that happened on the set of* Enter the Dragon.

According to witnesses, [a] man, aged about 20, appeared suddenly on the set. He told Lee he had seen him perform a lot of *Jeet Kune Do*, a form of martial art, on the screen and wanted to see it in real life. The witness said the man sneered when Lee set himself in a stance—and that was too much for the actor. He lashed out with a kick and the man fell. When he recovered and seemed anxious to have a crack at Lee he was dragged away by several members of the camera crew.

other martial arts films began entering theaters all over the country. Linda Lee writes:

As the craze for kung fu movies swept the world, Bruce stood alone at the top of the mountain, unquestionably the hottest property in show business. . . . With rapprochement [establishing a cordial relationship] between China and the United States a new factor in world politics, Bruce realized that his chance of becoming the first Chinese international superstar in history was no longer an impossible dream.[67]

The offer that Lee had been waiting for finally arrived in late 1972. Warner Brothers offered to coproduce a martial arts film with Lee and Chow. Fred Weintraub, a successful Hollywood producer, would be in charge of the project. The budget for the film would be more than eight hundred thousand dollars—an enormous sum at the time for a picture filmed in Hong Kong. "[The deal] was a staggering triumph for Bruce,"[68] said Linda Lee.

Bruce Lee knew that an American-produced and distributed film would give him international exposure. Finally, the realization of one of Lee's greatest ambitions was in front of him—he would have the chance to show a mass American audience his martial art. Lee and Chow agreed to coproduce the film, using their Concord production company. In early 1973, Lee stopped work on *The Game of Death* to devote his time to the new project, intending to come back to *The Game of Death* later.

ENTER THE DRAGON

The new American-produced film began shooting in February 1973. It would be called *Enter the Dragon*, and, even though Lee appeared in other movies released posthumously, it would be his last complete film.

The plot of *Enter the Dragon* involves Lee's character, a former student from the Shaolin temple in China, who is hired as a British secret agent to take part in a martial arts tournament being held on a private island off the coast of Hong Kong. Lee's mission is to flush out Han, another former Shaolin student, who runs the martial arts school on the island as a front for criminal activities. The film's action sequences, all choreographed by Lee, involve numerous martial arts duels, including those that are part of the tournament, as well as fights Lee's character encounters while searching for Han.

As with almost every other film Lee had worked on, *Enter the Dragon*'s production was fraught with troubles from the start. Numerous accidents occurred on the set, including one that left Lee with another severely cut hand. Additionally, fights arose repeatedly among the extra cast members, many of whom belonged to rival street gangs. Lee himself caused delays in shooting by twice walking off

Lee snaps the villain Han's knee backward in Enter the Dragon.

TROUBLE ON THE SET

Robert Clouse directed Enter the Dragon, *Bruce Lee's last and most successful film. In* Bruce Lee: A Biography, *Clouse describes some of the many troubles on the set.*

The stuntmen belonged to one of the many factions of Triads, the Chinese Mafia-like organization. It is one large group, but within that group are individual "families," each competing with the other. When we needed more stuntmen than one family could supply, we would have to call in the stuntmen from rival families, which led to near mortal fights. In any of the mass fights, such as the climactic encounter on the tournament field, the staged fight would quickly degenerate into a vengeful brawl. The fights did not necessarily stop when I yelled, "cut." In fact, the stage battle was just another excuse to maim one another. It was a cover and a screen to the bloodletting that occurred on a daily basis in Hong Kong.

the set because of creative disputes with director Robert Clouse and Chow, whom Lee thought was trying to take over the project.

Through the difficulties, Lee struggled to maintain control over every part of the film. He saw *Enter the Dragon* as the film that would make or break his career, particularly in the United States, and he was determined that it be filmed the way he wanted it. The quality of the film was so important to Lee

that he even threatened to quit the film because he felt he was losing control of the project.

Finally, in spite of all the problems and after ten grueling weeks of work, the film shoot finished. Lee watched an early pre-screening with pleasure, and when the lights came up he triumphantly punched the air. "This is the one!"[69] he exclaimed, convinced that *Enter the Dragon* would make him an international star.

7 Death by Misadventure

In the months before Bruce Lee's death in 1973, his friends and colleagues began noticing drastic changes in his behavior and appearance. Robert Clouse writes: "Many who had known him for years said he did not look well. They spoke of his weight loss and skin tone."[70] His usual focus and clarity were not there, and he suffered from mood swings. He also began lashing out at others without provocation. He exhibited erratic behavior and memory loss, asking the same question of someone again and again or repeating certain portions of a conversation. Further, even though he had abstained from using alcohol for most of his life, at this time he began drinking to excess on occasion and relied increasingly on painkillers and other drugs to alleviate his chronic back pain.

There is much controversy over the cause of these notable changes in Lee's personality. Some who knew Lee, such as Silliphant and his mother Grace, attribute the changes to the stresses of fame and to Lee's tendency to overwork in his pursuit of perfection. Others, such as biographer Tom Bleecker, claim that he had become addicted to painkillers and alcohol. Still oth-

ers, like biographer Bruce Thomas, speculate that the changes may have been early warnings of neurological problems. Whatever the cause of the changes in Lee's personality, though, they attracted negative public attention up to and beyond the time of his sudden death.

COLLAPSE

In the spring of 1973, following the filming of *Enter the Dragon*, Lee spent several days at Golden Harvest Studios in Hong Kong, dubbing the soundtrack for the film. On May 10, Lee sat in the cramped sound-proof booth recording dialogue for a scene. It was extremely hot in the studio as the air-conditioning could not run for fear of ruining the soundtrack recording, and Lee stepped out to get some air. When he did not return after almost a half hour, a member of the production staff went looking for him and found him unconscious in the bathroom.

Someone at the studio called an ambulance to take him to a nearby hospital, where an American physician saw that he was running a fever of 105 degrees Fahrenheit. Lee lapsed in and out of consciousness, periodically opening and closing his eyes, but his eyes would not focus. He was sweating profusely and having trouble breathing. The doctors assessed the possible causes of the collapse and found that fluid had built up around his brain, causing pressure. The condition, called cerebral edema, is very dangerous and can cause brain damage or death.

The doctors administered a drug to reduce the swelling around Lee's brain. Immediately after this, he went from

ON THE ILLUSION OF STARDOM

In this November 1971 interview with Bruce Lee by The Hong Kong Star *newspaper, published in* Bruce Lee: Words of the Dragon *(edited by John Little), Bruce Lee discusses fame. He believed that stardom was unimportant and an illusion, and that fame could be damaging and hard to live with.*

A "star" is an illusion. Man, is that something that can screw you up. When the public calls you a star, you had better know that it's only a game. If you believe and enjoy all those flatteries (yes, we are only human and we all do, to a certain extent), and forget the fact that the same people who once were your "pals" might just desert you to make friends with another "winner" the moment you no longer are, well, it's your choice.

Lee and the film Fist of Fury *became tremendously popular all over Asia.*

semicomatose into seizurelike convulsions, requiring the doctors to tape his arms and legs to the table so that he would not injure himself or those trying to help him. The doctors then waited for the drug to reduce the swelling, meanwhile preparing to do brain surgery if it became necessary. The hospital called Linda Lee, who came and waited by her husband's bedside.

After two hours, Bruce Lee opened his eyes. He was weak but over the next few hours he stabilized. Linda recalls that Bruce was scared and he had thought he was going to die. She says,

> [He told me] that he had, in fact felt very close to death—but that he could still exert his will and he had told himself "I'm going to fight it—I'm going to make it—I'm not going to give up" because he knew that if he thought any other way, he would die. Once or twice he mentioned, "Maybe that's the only place where I'll find peace." . . . When I heard him talk like this, it genuinely frightened me.[71]

Once Bruce was stable enough to be moved, Linda took her husband to Hong Kong's Queen Elizabeth Hospital. There he continued to improve, and further tests confirmed the diagnosis of cerebral edema.

Wanting more answers about Bruce's condition, Linda took him back to the United States to the UCLA (University of California Los Angeles) Hospital, one of the country's best medical facilities. There doctors ran extensive medical tests, but they could not find anything wrong with Bruce Lee. Bewildered

they gave Lee a clean bill of health and released him from the hospital.

BACK TO WORK

After his collapse, Lee decided that he and Linda would return to live in the United States after he finished filming his delayed project, *The Game of Death*. He considered the United States home, and wanted to begin working in America again. However, Lee hoped to return to Hong Kong at least once a year to make a movie because he knew he would have more control over the quality of the films there than he would in Hollywood.

While in Los Angeles, Lee finished dubbing *Enter the Dragon* at Warner Brothers. He also made several appearances on television to promote the film, including a spot on *The Tonight Show*. When all the work for *Enter the Dragon* was complete, he returned to Hong Kong with his family to finish *The Game of Death*.

BAD PUBLICITY

When Lee arrived in Hong Kong, he discovered that the local newspapers were speculating wildly about his collapse and about his personal and professional life. Although some of the stories were true (albeit often distorted), most were outright fabrications.

In the beginning of his career, the Hong Kong media had been almost unanimously kind to Lee because he was a new star and a hero to so many Hong Kong Chinese. But,

Bruce Lee in a scene from The Game of Death. *While working on that movie, Lee had to deal with rumors and bad press.*

as his wealth and fame increased, many newspapers tried to ruin his reputation. When Yip Man died during the filming of *Enter the Dragon,* for instance, and Lee was unable to attend the funeral because of a tight film schedule, several newspapers claimed that he was disrespectful and without honor. This was a significant insult because Chinese culture highly values respect and honor, particularly for parents and teachers. Numerous articles also printed rumors that Lee was involved in extramarital relationships. These stories specifically focused on Lee's relationship with the female lead actress in *The Game of Death,* Betty Ting Pei, with whom Lee was spending a great deal of time. Even stories prematurely proclaiming his death became so commonplace that his friends and family finally could not trust the news.

CONFRONTING LO WEI

One of Lee's most well-known publicity scandals happened only two weeks before his death, when he confronted and reportedly threatened the life of director Lo Wei. The two men had gotten along poorly when they worked together on *The Big Boss* and *Fist of Fury.* Lee had no respect for the director and believed Lo Wei cared little about the quality of the films he worked on.

Although the men had not worked together for more than a year, Lee's animosity toward Lo Wei had not subsided since filming the two movies. Lo Wei had capitalized on Lee's success, becoming a millionaire from the films, and publicly claimed to have taught Lee how to fight.

On July 10, 1973, while working on *The Game of Death,* Lee heard that Lo Wei was in the same studio screening a film. Lee burst into the screening room, reportedly brandishing a knife, and threatened to kill the director. The police were called, and even though they did not find a knife, they sided with Lo Wei. However, instead of arresting Lee, they made him sign a statement declaring he would stay away from Lo Wei from then on.

That evening Lee appeared on a popular Hong Kong talk show called *Enjoy Yourself Tonight.* The host inquired about the incident with Lo Wei, and Lee admitted to the confrontation but not the weapon charge. He said, "If I want to kill Low Wei, I would not use a knife. Two fingers would be enough."[72] The host asked Lee to demonstrate what he meant, and Lee agreed. Using the host as his "victim," Lee executed a simple shoulder push with two fingers that knocked the host back several feet and onto the floor.

No matter what the truth was about the alleged assault on Lo Wei, the press reported only the director's side of the story, saying that Lee had become arrogant and dangerous. Further, newspaper reports cited the demonstration on *Enjoy Yourself Tonight* as an assault on the host.

July 20, 1973

Because of the press's pernicious attitude toward Lee at the end of his life, reports concerning the events surrounding his death became a source of controversy. Rumors and speculation about what really happened the day Lee died are still published. But the people who had contact with Lee on the day he died—Linda Lee, Raymond Chow, and actress Betty Ting Pei, say that, up until that evening, there was nothing out of the ordinary about Lee's behavior or about the events of the day.

Early on July 20, 1973, while Linda was getting ready to leave for lunch with a friend, Bruce was in the study of their home in Kowloon. Bruce told Linda that Chow was going to come over to talk about script ideas for *The Game of Death*, and the two

Bruce Lee died on July 20, 1973.

men would be having dinner that evening with Pei and George Lazenby, a British actor Lee wanted to cast.

That afternoon, after Chow and Lee finished their work at Lee's house, Chow dropped Lee off at Pei's apartment, where she and Lee worked together on the script for a couple of hours. Lee complained of a headache and Pei gave him a tablet of Equagesic, a prescription headache drug, which had been given to her by her doctor.

Around 7:30 P.M., Lee told Pei he did not feel well and went to lie down in the bedroom. A little later, Chow phoned Pei's apartment from the restaurant where he and Lazenby were waiting for Pei and Lee. Chow asked why she and Lee were late for dinner. Pei went to the bedroom to wake Lee but he would not wake up. Worried, Chow returned to Pei's apartment to try to wake Lee but also could not. Pei and Chow called a doctor, who spent ten minutes trying to revive Lee. When the doctor could not get Lee to respond, he rushed him by ambulance to Queen Elizabeth Hospital.

Chow also called Linda Lee and told her to meet him at the hospital. Linda arrived at the hospital before Bruce's ambulance. At first she thought that Chow's call had been a joke or a hoax. She recalls:

> I arrived at the hospital about 15 minutes before the ambulance, but at first it seemed as if there had been some mistake. When I inquired about Bruce, the man at the desk suggested, "Somebody must have been joking—we don't know anything about it." This didn't seem completely implausible, since many extraordinary events characterized our

lives in Hong Kong. I had thought it was Raymond's voice on the phone, but perhaps I was being fooled. I was within seconds of calling home where I fully expected Bruce to be, wondering where I was. Then the ambulance arrived. . . . [Bruce] was wheeled into an emergency ward where a team began massaging his heart. It never occurred to me that he might die, let alone that he might already be dead.[73]

The doctors made numerous attempts to revive Bruce Lee, but they could not save him.

MEDIA CIRCUS

When news broke of Bruce Lee's death, many of his friends and family members did not believe it. Over the past months, newspapers had fabricated stories about Lee's death to sell papers. There had been so many false reports that many people close to Lee assumed this was just another one. According to Bruce Thomas, even Grace Lee did not believe the news of her son's death at first:

> For months, stories had been appearing in the Hong Kong press saying that he was dead. She would immediately call up the paper or magazine to see if it was true; it never was. When she told Bruce how much the stories upset her, he would explain the obvious: that they were simply lies to sell magazines. He told her the next time she heard or read such a story not to believe it. When one of Grace Lee's friends called her, crying, with the news that Bruce was dead she told her friend that it was a lie.[74]

Lee's success in films like Fist of Fury *(pictured) made him susceptible to rumors. Even after he died, rumors about the events surrounding his death abounded.*

Once it became clear that the reports of Bruce Lee's death were true, rumors and speculation spread through the media about the circumstances surrounding his death. For months and years afterward, the media and people who had known or worked with Lee proffered numerous theories. These ranged from overwork to murder by a jealous mistress or assassination by ninjas in retaliation for Lee's flaunting of Chinese tradition over the years.

The rumors were fueled by two suspicious events following Lee's death. First, trying to protect Lee's reputation against rumors of infidelity, Chow conspired to hide Lee's whereabouts at the time of his death, circulating a false story that he had died at home instead of Pei's apartment. When a journalist who checked the ambulance records exposed the lie and discovered that Lee had been at the home of Pei, Pei also lied, saying that she had not been home at the time of Lee's death. "The lie spawned banner headlines," writes Robert Clouse, "and created a controversy which remains today. The episode fed more and more rumors and led to more and more denials, becoming a treasure trove for marauding news hounds."[75]

Bruce Lee had two funerals, one in Hong Kong and one in Seattle.

FUNERALS FOR A DRAGON

Even though the media had tried to ruin Lee's reputation, it was clear that he was loved and respected by many Hong Kong Chinese. Thirty thousand mourners gathered outside his memorial service at the Kowloon Funeral Parlor in Hong Kong on July 25, 1973. The service was held in lieu of a funeral, as Linda Lee had decided to bury his body in the United States, fearing that if the body were buried in Hong Kong future political upheaval might someday make it impossible for her to visit the grave. Bruce Lee's body, dressed in a blue suit, lay in an open bronze casket. Linda Lee and her children Brandon and Shannon, dressed in traditional white Chinese mourning garments, sat near the casket as the mourners filed past.

The next day, Linda Lee and her children left with Bruce Lee's body for Seattle, where he was buried on July 31, 1973, in Lake View Cemetery. At the funeral, Linda Lee eulogized her husband. She said, "He lived every day as a day of discovery. His thirty-two years were full of living."[76]

INQUEST

The rumors about the cause and nature of Lee's death received so much attention that the Hong Kong government called for an investigation. Linda Lee flew to Hong Kong and spent six weeks attending the inquest, which began on September 3, 1973. She listened as the various rumors and theories about Lee's death were presented to the court, not believing any of them. She writes:

> I listened to the fanciful theories and heard the speculations grow. The more closely one analyzed these ideas, the more absurd they seemed. They ranged from suggestions that Run Run Shaw had Bruce murdered to suggestions that Raymond Chow had organized it. The truth was that the people of Hong Kong had lost a great hero and were reluctant to accept the reality that their super-hero could succumb as easily as any other mortal.[77]

After the theories were presented, the British government forensic laboratory carried out an autopsy. They found evidence of a severe swelling around Lee's brain. They found no evidence of poisoning or other foul play. Ultimately, investigators concluded that Lee had been killed by an acute cerebral edema due to an unusual hypersensitivity to the Equagesic tablet. The British court ruled that Lee's death was death by misadventure (an accidental death).

Even after the inquest, the press did not stop speculating. Linda Lee writes: "Amid the onrush of rumors, counter-rumors, and lurid assertions, I publicly pleaded to the people of Hong Kong and the world to let the matter alone. . . . No one, I'm sorry to say, seemed to be listening."[78]

THE DRAGON LIVES

The rumors and speculation about the death of Bruce Lee have never completely died out, but neither have his more positive legacies. Lee's popularity continues to grow. Journalist Judith Rosen writes:

> Nearly three decades after his death . . . Bruce Lee's popularity continues . . . to grow. . . . Lee is the subject of numerous Web sites—more than 55—many of them claiming Lee "sightings." When *Premiere* magazine searched the Web

---

EULOGY FOR A TEACHER AND FRIEND

Quoted in The Bruce Lee Story, *by Linda Lee, actor James Coburn gave this brief eulogy for his friend and teacher at Bruce Lee's funeral in Seattle.*

Farewell brother. It has been an honor to share this space in time with you. As a friend and as a teacher, you have . . . brought my physical, spiritual, and psychological selves together. Thank you. May peace be with you.

last May to compile its e-list of the top 10 movie actors, Lee was number nine—ahead of George Clooney. A recent article in *Time* magazine singled out Lee, along with Mother Teresa and Jackie Robinson as one of the 20 most courageous people of the past century.[79]

At the time of his death, Bruce Lee was the highest paid movie star in the world. Although he did not live to see it, the Los Angeles premiere of *Enter the Dragon* in 1973 was an enormous success. The movie would go on to make more than $200 million worldwide. "Considering the ratio of money invested [in making the film] to the money it earned," writes Robert Clouse, "it has to be one of the most profitable pictures ever made."[80]

Lee kicks at a Japanese man in Enter the Dragon. *It was his last film and one of the most profitable films ever made.*

A 2000 exhibit highlights artwork of Bruce Lee. Despite his death, Lee remains one of the world's most famous celebrities.

Even since Lee's death, filmmakers have continued to produce Bruce Lee films. Raymond Chow and Robert Clouse completed *The Game of Death* in 1978 by splicing the twenty minutes of film Lee had shot before his death with new footage starring a Bruce Lee double. In 1982, Golden Harvest again used Lee's original twenty minutes to make *The Game of Death II*. Both films grossed large sums of money at the box office because of Lee's popularity and the quality of his films. In 2001, Lee's family agreed to plans for a new Bruce Lee film called

Dragon Warrior, which will star a completely computer-generated version of Bruce Lee.

Beyond the success of his films, Bruce Lee's name sells countless magazines and books. Memorabilia bearing his name or face are widely available. There are even Bruce Lee fan clubs and conventions.

CONTRIBUTION TO THE FUTURE

Apart from his celebrity and icon status, Bruce Lee brought kung fu to the West and was responsible for its popularity. He dramatically changed the martial arts world, also leaving his writings on *jeet kune do,* which are now studied at many martial arts schools all over the world.

Finally, Bruce Lee left his example. His career pioneered the way in Hollywood for other Asian and Asian American actors and martial artists by assuring producers and studios that films starring Asians can be successful in America. And in the Hong Kong film industry, he broke the traditional mold, setting new standards for quality, creative freedom, and upward mobility in salary. His contributions to martial arts and films continue to entertain and influence new generations of martial arts students, film audiences, and Bruce Lee fans.

Notes

Chapter 1: Enter the Dragon

1. Tom Bleecker, *Unsettled Matters: The Life and Death of Bruce Lee.* Lompoc, CA: Gilderoy Publications, 1996, p. 18.

2. Quoted in Bruce Thomas, *Bruce Lee: Fighting Spirit.* Berkeley, CA: Frog, 1994, p. 8.

3. Linda Lee, *The Bruce Lee Story.* Santa Clarita, CA: Ohara Publications, 1989, p. 22.

4. Quoted in Thomas, *Bruce Lee: Fighting Spirit,* p. 14.

5. Robert Clouse, *Bruce Lee: The Biography.* Burbank, CA: Unique Publications, 1988, p. 19.

6. Quoted in Thomas, *Bruce Lee: Fighting Spirit,* p. 21.

7. Quoted in Bleecker, *Unsettled Matters,* p. 23.

8. Quoted in Lee, *The Bruce Lee Story,* p. 26.

9. Bleecker, *Unsettled Matters,* p. 26.

10. Lee, *The Bruce Lee Story,* p. 31.

Chapter 2: The Seattle Years

11. Lee, *The Bruce Lee Story,* p. 41.

12. Quoted in Thomas, *Bruce Lee: Fighting Spirit,* p. 33.

13. Quoted in John Little, ed., *Bruce Lee: Letters of the Dragon: Correspondence, 1958–1973.* Boston: Tuttle Publishing, 1998, p. 25.

14. Thomas, *Bruce Lee: Fighting Spirit,* p. 34.

15. Thomas, *Bruce Lee: Fighting Spirit,* pp. 41–42.

16. Quoted in Little, *Bruce Lee: Letters of the Dragon,* pp. 30–31.

17. Quoted in Bleecker, *Unsettled Matters,* p. 34.

18. Quoted in Bleecker, *Unsettled Matters,* p. 35.

19. Quoted in Bleecker, *Unsettled Matters,* p. 35.

20. Quoted in Bleecker, *Unsettled Matters,* p. 37.

21. Lee, *The Bruce Lee Story,* pp. 11–12.

22. Lee, *The Bruce Lee Story,* p. 16.

23. Lee, *The Bruce Lee Story,* p. 16.

Chapter 3: Discovered!

24. Clouse, *Bruce Lee: The Biography,* pp. 56–57.

25. Quoted in Thomas, *Bruce Lee: Fighting Spirit,* p. 57.

26. Quoted in Thomas, *Bruce Lee: Fighting Spirit,* p. 58.

27. Quoted in Thomas, *Bruce Lee: Fighting Spirit,* p. 58.

28. Lee, *The Bruce Lee Story,* p. 18.

29. Lee, *The Bruce Lee Story,* p. 19.

30. Quoted in Clouse, *Bruce Lee: The Biography,* p. 55.

31. Quoted in Clouse, *Bruce Lee: The Biography,* p. 56.

32. Lee, *The Bruce Lee Story,* p. 19.

33. Quoted in Lee, *The Bruce Lee Story,* p. 52.

34. Lee, *The Bruce Lee Story,* p. 52.

35. Lee, *The Bruce Lee Story,* p. 53.

36. Thomas, *Bruce Lee: Fighting Spirit,* pp. 69–71.

37. Lee, *The Bruce Lee Story,* p. 72.

Chapter 4: Hollywood

38. Lee, *The Bruce Lee Story,* p. 73.

39. Quoted in Little, *Bruce Lee: Letters of the Dragon,* pp. 77–78.

40. Lee, *The Bruce Lee Story,* p. 75.

41. Quoted in Thomas, *Bruce Lee: Fighting Spirit,* pp. 93–94.

42. Quoted in Clouse, *Bruce Lee: The Biography,* p. 70.

43. Lee, *The Bruce Lee Story*, p. 88.

44. Lee, *The Bruce Lee Story*, pp. 88–89.

45. Quoted in Little, *Bruce Lee: Letters of the Dragon*, pp. 110–11.

Chapter 5: Breaking Through

46. Thomas, *Bruce Lee: Fighting Spirit*, p. 107.

47. Clouse, *Bruce Lee: The Biography*, p. 70.

48. Lee, *The Bruce Lee Story*, p. 95.

49. Thomas, *Bruce Lee: Fighting Spirit*, p. 108.

50. Quoted in Clouse, *Bruce Lee: The Biography*, p. 84.

51. Quoted in Clouse, *Bruce Lee: The Biography*, p. 87.

52. Quoted in Clouse, *Bruce Lee: The Biography*, p. 90.

53. Quoted in John Little, ed., *Striking Thoughts: Bruce Lee's Wisdom for Daily Living.* Boston: Tuttle Publishing, 2000, pp.98–99.

54. Lee, *The Bruce Lee Story*, p. 80.

55. Quoted in Lee, *The Bruce Lee Story*, p. 96.

56. Lee, *The Bruce Lee Story*, p. 100.

57. Lee, *The Bruce Lee Story*, p. 100.

58. Quoted in Lee, *The Bruce Lee Story*, p. 101.

Chapter 6: King of Hong Kong

59. Quoted in Little, *Bruce Lee: Letters of the Dragon*, pp. 148–49.

60. Thomas, *Bruce Lee: Fighting Spirit*, pp. 127–28.

61. Clouse, *Bruce Lee: The Biography*, p. 101.

62. Lee, *The Bruce Lee Story*, p. 107.

63. Clouse, *Bruce Lee: The Biography*, p. 102.

64. Thomas, *Bruce Lee: Fighting Spirit*, p. 138.

65. Quoted in Lee, *The Bruce Lee Story*, p. 118.

66. Lee, *The Bruce Lee Story*, p. 125.

67. Lee, *The Bruce Lee Story*, p. 135.

68. Lee, *The Bruce Lee Story*, p. 135.

69. Quoted in Thomas, *Bruce Lee: Fighting Spirit*, p. 191.

Chapter 7: Death by Misadventure

70. Clouse, *Bruce Lee: The Biography*, p. 152.

71. Lee, *The Bruce Lee Story*, p. 153.

72. Quoted in Clouse, *Bruce Lee: The Biography*, p. 176.

73. Lee, *The Bruce Lee Story*, p. 157.

74. Thomas, *Bruce Lee: Fighting Spirit*, p. 204.

75. Clouse, *Bruce Lee: The Biography*, p. 183.

76. Quoted in Thomas, *Bruce Lee: Fighting Spirit*, p. 207.

77. Lee, *The Bruce Lee Story*, pp. 162–63.

78. Lee, *The Bruce Lee Story*, p. 163.

79. Judith Rosen, "Bruce Lee Kicks into High Gear," *Publisher's Weekly*, November 6, 2000, p. 30.

80. Clouse, *Bruce Lee: The Biography*, p. 161.

For Further Reading

James Bishop, *Remembering Bruce: The Enduring Legacy of the Martial Arts Superstar.* Nipomo, CA: Cyclone Books, 1999. A glowing biography written by a young Bruce Lee fan, containing many interviews and stories from people who knew and studied with Lee. Focuses on Lee's martial arts career rather than his personal life.

Jon E. Lewis, *They Died Too Young: Bruce Lee.* Philadelphia: Chelsea Publications, 1998. Very brief biography written for young adults.

Linda Tagliaferro, *Bruce Lee.* Minneapolis: Lerner Publications, 2000. Short, straightforward biography written with the cooperation of the Bruce Lee estate.

Unique Publications, *Bruce Lee: The Untold Story.* Burbank, CA: Unique Publications, 1986. Good, short biographical chronology of Bruce Lee's life accompanied by numerous pictures. Not written specifically for young adults or children.

Works Consulted

Books

Alan Birch, *Hong Kong: The Colony that Never Was*. Hong Kong: The Guidebook Company, 1991. Pictorial and journalistic account of Hong Kong's history as a colony under the British and its occupation by Japan in 1941.

Tom Bleecker, *Unsettled Matters: The Life and Death of Bruce Lee*. Lompoc, CA: Gilderoy Publications, 1996. Written by Linda Lee's ex-husband, this biography includes a lot of speculative detail into the life of Bruce Lee. Contains some factual inaccuracies and sensationalism.

Louis Chunovic, *Bruce Lee: The Tao of the Dragon Warrior*. New York: St. Martin's Griffin, 1996. Short biography with many pictures, written in cooperation with the Bruce Lee estate. Includes foreword by Linda Lee Cadwell.

Robert Clouse, *Bruce Lee: The Biography*. Burbank, CA: Unique Publications, 1988. Good biography of Bruce Lee from Robert Clouse, director of *Enter the Dragon*. Includes numerous black and white pictures not found in other biographies.

Kung Fu Monthly, The Unbeatable Bruce Lee: A Manual of the Master in Action. Seacaucus, NJ: Castle Books, 1978. Step-by-step pictorial and illustrated instruction manual of Bruce Lee's martial arts styles compiled by *Kung Fu Monthly* magazine.

Linda Lee, *The Bruce Lee Story*. Santa Clarita, CA: Ohara Publications, 1989. Fond biography by Bruce Lee's widow (who now goes by the name of Linda Lee Cadwell) containing many insights into his personal character. Includes many good pictures of Bruce Lee, his family, and his friends.

John Little, ed., *Bruce Lee: Artist of Life*. Boston: Tuttle Publishing, 1999. Collection of writings from Bruce Lee, including poetry, philosophy, and martial arts instruction.

———, *Bruce Lee: Jeet Kune Do: Bruce Lee's Commentaries on the Martial Way*. Boston: Tuttle Publishing, 1997. Detailed, illustrated writings concerning the philosophical and technical practice of Bruce Lee's martial art, *jeet kune do* (way of the intercepting fist).

———, *Bruce Lee: Letters of the Dragon: Correspondence, 1958–1973*. Boston: Tuttle Publishing, 1998. Selective compilation of Bruce Lee's correspondence, complete with illustrations Lee included in his letters and supplemental photographs supplied by his widow, Linda Lee Cadwell.

———, *Bruce Lee: The Tao of Gung Fu: A Study in the Way of Chinese Martial Art*. Boston: Tuttle Publishing, 1997. Writings, illustrations, and philosophies on *gung fu* taken from the estate of Bruce Lee.

———, *Bruce Lee: Words of the Dragon: Interviews 1958–1973*. Boston: Tuttle Publishing, 1997. A collection of newspaper clippings, magazine articles, and interview transcripts with Bruce Lee. Usefully footnoted.

———, *Striking Thoughts: Bruce Lee's Wisdom for Daily Living*. Boston: Tuttle Publishing, 2000. Aphorisms, philosophies, and meditative writings on various topics compiled from Lee's personal and school papers.

Davis Miller, *The Tao of Bruce Lee: A Martial Arts Memoir*. New York: Harmony Books, 2000. Part memoir, part biography, Miller uses his personal experiences with martial arts as a touchstone to examine the life and death of Bruce Lee.

Bruce Thomas, *Bruce Lee: Fighting Spirit*. Berkeley, CA: Frog, 1994. Excellent, serious biography of Bruce Lee's life, including in-depth explorations of the influences and details of his martial arts practice. Includes good appendices.

Periodicals

Tim Appelo, "Tears of the Dragon," *Entertainment Weekly*, May 14, 1993.

Entertainment Weekly, "Exit the Dragon," *Entertainment Weekly*, July 17, 1998.

Frank Lovece, "Faux Lee Artists," *Entertainment Weekly*, May 7, 1993.

People Weekly, "Enter the Son of the Dragon," *People Weekly*, February 3, 1986.

Erin Richter, "The Son Also Sets," *Entertainment Weekly*, April 7, 2000.

Judith Rosen, "Bruce Lee Kicks into High Gear," *Publisher's Weekly*, November 6, 2000.

Betsy Sharkey, "Fate's Children: Bruce and Brandon," *New York Times*, May 2, 1993.

Joel Stein, "The Gladiator," *Time*, June 14, 1999.

Websites

Hong Kong '97: Lives in Transition (www.pbs.org/pov/hongkong). PBS provides an on-line timeline and history of Hong Kong from its colonization by the British up to 1997.

Videos

The Big Boss (U.S. title: *Fists of Fury*), Golden Harvest Studios, 1971. Bruce Lee stars as a man who must break a solemn vow to avoid fighting in order to avenge the murder of his teacher by drug smugglers.

Bruce Lee: The Immortal Dragon, A&E Biography, 1996. Good overview documentary on the life of Bruce Lee, including interviews with his friends and family and footage from his 1965 screen test.

Circle of Iron, New World Pictures, 1979. Filmed in Israel, this martial arts film is loosely based on the screenplay of *The Silent Flute* developed by Bruce Lee, James Coburn, and Stirling Silliphant. It stars David Carradine as a man on an eternal quest for truth.

Dragon: The Bruce Lee Story, Universal Pictures, 1993. In this supposedly biographical motion picture, Bruce Lee is played by Jason Scott Lee (no relation). The story, loosely based on the book by Lee's widow, Linda Lee Cadwell, *Bruce Lee: The Man Only I Knew*, ostensibly follows Bruce Lee's life and career, but the film is widely panned by biographers as inaccurate and sensationalistic.

Enter the Dragon, Warner Brothers, 1973. In the American film that made him world famous, released just months after his death, Bruce Lee stars as a man recruited by British intelligence to search for an opium smuggler on an island off the coast of Hong Kong.

Fist of Fury (U.S. title: *The Chinese Connection*), Golden Harvest Studios, 1971. Bruce Lee stars as a man who must survive a mob organization's attempts to kill him. After the organization kills his mother, he returns to battle and finally defeats the leader of the organization himself.

The Game of Death, Golden Harvest Studios, 1979. Only half-finished upon Bruce Lee's death and released posthumously using outtakes and a double, *The Game of Death* is a thriller about a young martial arts movie star who gets involved with the Chinese crime syndicate.

Marlowe, MGM, 1969. Stirling Silliphant wrote the screenplay adaptation of Raymond Chandler's *The Little Sister*. James Garner stars as detective Philip Marlowe, whose investigation is complicated by Bruce Lee's kung fu villain, Winslow Wong. Bruce Lee's American feature film debut.

The Way of the Dragon, Concord (alternate title: *Return of the Dragon*), 1973. In his directorial and screenwriting debut, Bruce Lee also stars as "Lee," a man who fights on behalf of an owner of a Chinese restaurant in Rome. Includes the second appearance on film of Chuck Norris, Bruce Lee's friend and student.

Index

Abdul-Jabbar, Kareem, 62, 96
Ali, Muhammad, 69

Batman (television series), 53, 60
Bel Air, California, 67
Big Boss, The (film), 84–89, 91, 104
Black Beauty (car), 58
Black Belt (magazine), 91–92
Bleecker, Tom, 17, 26, 37, 44, 100
Blondie (television series), 62
Bobo (Bruce's dog), 51
boxing, 26
Bruce Lee: Fighting Spirit (Thomas), 27, 38, 51, 60, 63, 93
Bruce Lee: Letters of the Dragon: Correspondence, 1958–1973 (Little), 54
Bruce Lee: The Biography (Clouse), 32, 64, 99
Bruce Lee: Words of the Dragon (Little), 20, 69, 75, 82, 97, 101
Bruce Lee Story, The (Linda Lee), 23–24, 87, 109

Caine, 71
Carradine, David, 71–72, 78–79
Chandler, Raymond, 66

Charlie Chan (radio program), 52–53
Cheng Chao An, 84
Cheung, Hawkins, 27
Cheung, William, 22, 70
China Mail (newspaper), 82, 97
Chinatown (San Francisco), 14–15
Chinese Youth Club, 33
Chow, Raymond
    clashes with Bruce, 99
    completes production of The Game of Death, 111
    last visit with Bruce, 105–106
    makes movie offers to Bruce, 81, 83, 88–89
    production company partnership with Bruce and, 92, 95
Chow, Ruby, 29–32
Chow Ping, 29–30
Clouse, Robert
    on Bruce fighting as youngster, 23
    on Bruce's behavioral changes before his death, 100
    on Bruce's merciless drive, 64
    on Bruce's popularity with stuntmen, 85–86
    on Bruce's problems on set of Enter the Dragon, 99

on Bruce's reaction to Kung Fu casting, 71
    on Bruce's relationship with Ruby Chow, 32
    on Chinese audience's response to The Big Boss, 87
    clashes with Lee on Enter the Dragon, 99
    completes production of The Game of Death, 111
    describes James Lee, 43
    on Pei lying to media about Bruce's death, 107
    on popularity of Enter the Dragon, 110
Coburn, James, 62, 76–78, 88, 109
Concord (production company), 92, 95, 97
Crow, The (film), 56
Crown Colony Cha-Cha Championship, 23

Damone, Vic, 63
DeMile, James, 31, 35
Denes, Gyula, 33
Dozier, William, 45, 52–53, 56, 59–60
Dragon Warrior (film), 111
Draven, Eric, 56

Edison Technical School, 30–31, 35

Emery, Linda. *See* Lee, Linda

Enjoy Yourself Tonight (television program), 104

Entertainment Weekly (magazine), 56

Enter the Dragon (film), 12, 97–100, 102–103, 110

Fist of Fury (film), 88–91, 104

Fists of Fury (film), 84, 87

FitzSimmons, Charles, 62

Frazier, Joe, 69

Game of Death, The (film), 95–96, 102–105, 111

Game of Death II, The (film), 111

Garner, James, 66

Golden Harvest Studios, 75, 81, 84, 89, 92, 100, 111

Green Hornet, The (television series), 53–54, 57–60, 71

gung fu. *See* kung fu

Gunsmoke (television series), 45

Han, 98

Here Come the Brides (television series), 62

Hill, Napoleon, 33

Hong Kong
   Bruce's childhood in, 15–19, 25–26, 28
   filming of *The Big Boss* in, 84–89

investigation of Bruce's death in, 109
   popularity of Bruce in, 72–73, 81, 86–91

Hong Kong Star (newspaper), 75, 101

Immigration Act of 1940, 14

India, 76–78

Inosanto, Dan, 45, 60, 96

International District (Seattle), 29, 32

International Karate Tournament, 43, 52

Ironside (television series), 62

Jackson, Herb, 52

Japan
   attacks Pearl Harbor, 16

jeet kune do, 13, 69–70, 80, 95–96

Jun Fan Gung Fu Institute, 39, 41, 43, 61

Kato, 53, 57–60

Kimura, Taky, 39, 41, 48

Kowloon, Hong Kong, 23, 26, 89

kung fu, 21–24, 27, 31, 34–35, 37, 39–40

Kung Fu (television series), 71–72, 74, 79

La Salle College, 19, 25

Las Vegas, Nevada, 63

Lazenby, George, 106

Lee, Agnes (sister), 17, 54

Lee, Brandon Bruce (son), 52–54, 56, 72–73, 89, 108

Lee, Bruce
   birth of, 14
   challenged by Wong Jack Man, 49–51
   childhood of, 16–20
   collapses on set of *Enter the Dragon*, 100–102
   death of, 33–34, 106
   develops *jeet kune do*, 69–70
   dreams of establishing kung fu school, 34–35
   education of, 18–19, 25, 30–31
   exiled from Hong Kong, 26, 28
   on fame, 92, 101
   film and television appearances by, 62
      in Cantonese-language films, 19
      see also names of specific films and television shows
   injures back during morning workout, 67–68
   learns *wing chun*, 22–24
   marries Linda, 45–48
   moves to Oakland, 42–43
   partnership in Concord, 92–93
   personality of, 18–20, 33–35, 44
   popularity of in Hong Kong, 72–73, 86–89
   in Seattle

dates Linda, 38–42
dates Sanbo, 35–38
opens Jun Fan Gung
    Fu Institute, 39
teaches *wing chun* in,
    31–33
works in Chinese
    restaurant, 29–31
takes screen test in Los
    Angeles, 52–53
teaches martial arts to
    celebrities, 62
on violence in kung fu
    films, 82
wins Crown Colony
    Cha-Cha
    Championship, 23
wins 1958 Boxing
    Championship, 26
writes and produces
    The Silent Flute, 74,
    76–79
Lee, Grace (mother)
on changes in Bruce's
    personality, 100
encourages Bruce to
    leave Hong Kong, 26
faces discipline
    problems with Bruce,
    18–19
gives affection to
    Brandon, 54
gives birth to Bruce,
    14–15
moves to America, 72
objects to Bruce fighting
    other teenagers, 21
reacts to Bruce's death,
    106

Lee, James, 41, 43, 48, 52
Lee, Jun Fan. *See* Lee,
    Bruce
Lee (Li), Hoi Chuen
    (father), 14–15, 17–18,
    21, 53
Lee, Linda (wife)
attends Bruce's funeral,
    108
attends premiere of *The
    Big Boss*, 86–87
on Bruce becoming first
    Chinese international
    superstar, 97
on Bruce's enjoyment of
    celebrity status, 60
on Bruce's expectations
    of commitment on
    The Way of the Dragon,
    94–95
on Bruce's grades in
    college, 19
on Bruce's parents
    exiling him from
    Hong Kong, 26, 28
on Bruce's problem
    with insomnia, 104
on Bruce's reaction to
    collapse, 102
on Bruce's reaction to
    failure, 80
on challenge by Wong
    Jack Man, 49–51
dates Bruce, 38–42
describes Bruce's early
    dating years, 23
on investigation into
    Bruce's death, 109
on life in Hollywood,
    67

marries Bruce, 45–48
recalls Bruce's death,
    106
on stereotyping
    Chinese, 59
visits Bruce's parents in
    Hong Kong, 53–55, 57
works to support
    family, 68, 70–71
Lee, Peter (brother), 14,
    17
Lee, Phoebe (sister), 14,
    17
Lee, Robert (brother), 17,
    25, 33
Lee, Shannon (daughter),
    67, 108
Lewis, Joe, 62
Little, John, 20, 54, 75, 82,
    97, 101
Little Sister, The
    (Chandler), 66
Longstreet (television
    series), 80–81, 86, 92
Lo Wei, 85, 89, 92, 104

Maltz, Maxwell, 33
Manchu dynasty, 22
Marlowe (film), 66
Marvin, Lee, 62
McQueen, Steve, 62, 74,
    76
Mo Si Tung. *See* Lee,
    Bruce

National Broadcasting
    Company (NBC), 71
National Karate
    Championship, 61–62

NBC. *See* National Broadcasting Company
Ngan, Wu (brother), 17
Ng Mui, 22
1958 Boxing Championship, 26
Norris, Chuck, 62, 94, 96

Oakland, California, 42, 43, 48
Orphan, The (film), 19

Pak Chong, 83–84
Palmer, Doug, 38
Parker, Ed, 43
Peale, Norman Vincent, 33
Pearl Harbor, 16
Pei, Betty Ting, 103, 105–107
Perry Mason (television series), 45

Queen Elizabeth Hospital, 102

Reid, Britt, 58–59
Richter, Erin, 56
Roethke, Theodore, 37
Roosevelt, Franklin, 14
Rosen, Judith, 109–10
Ruby Chow's Chinese Restaurant, 29–32

Saint Francis Xavier College, 25–26
San Francisco, California, 14–15, 29–30
Sanbo, Amy, 35–37
Seattle
  Bruce's girlfriends in, 35–42
  Bruce teaches *wing chun* in, 31–33
  Bruce works in Chinese restaurant in, 29–31
Seattle Congregational Church, 48
Seattle Times (newspaper), 31
Sebring, Jay, 45, 62
Shaw, Run Run, 73–74, 81, 88–89
Silent Flute, The (film), 74, 76–79
Silliphant, Stirling, 62, 64–65, 71, 76–78, 80–81, 100
Sound of Music, The (film), 88
Space Needle (Seattle), 40
Stone, Mike, 62
Stone, W. Clement, 33
street fights, 26
Sui, Uncle, 27
superstitions, 14

Tang Lung, 93
Thomas, Bruce
  on Bruce as a quick study, 27
  on Bruce meeting Damone in Las Vegas, 63
  on Bruce's ability to get acting jobs, 71
  on Bruce's inspiration behind *The Silent Flute*, 74
  on Bruce's kung fu demonstration with DeMile, 31
  on Bruce's nightmare, 33–34
  on Bruce's screen test, 52–53
  on Bruce's status as public figure in Hong Kong, 90–91
  on changes in Bruce's personality before his death, 100
  describes Bruce's fitness program, 51
  describes one of Bruce's and Palmer's practical jokes, 38
  describes purpose of one-inch punch, 45
  on end of friendship with Unicorn, 93
  on Grace's reaction to Bruce's death, 106
  on Inosanto's friendship with Bruce, 60
  on Lo Wei's lack of attention to *The Big Boss*, 85
Thomas Crown Affair, The (film), 74
Tigers, 19, 21
Tonight Show, The (television program), 102
Twentieth-Century Fox, 45, 52

Unicorn, 93
Unicorn Palm, The (film), 93
University of California Los Angeles (UCLA) Hospital, 102

University of Washington (UW), 35, 37–38

Unsettled Matters: The Life and Death of Bruce Lee (Bleecker), 37, 44

UW. *See* University of Washington

Walk in the Spring Rain, A (film), 64–65

Warner Brothers, 102

Warrior, The. See Kung Fu

Way of the Dragon, The (film), 93–95

"Way of the Intercepting Fist, The," 80

Williams, Van, 58

wing chun, 22–24, 27, 31, 70

Wong Jack Man, 49–51, 69

Wong, Winslow, 66

World War II, 15–16, 30, 90

Wrecking Crew, The (film), 64

Yan, Pak, 38

Yip Man, 21–24, 103

Young, Fook, 33

Picture Credits

About the Author

Andy Koopmans's short stories, poetry, and essays have appeared in literary journals across the United States. He lives in Seattle, Washington, with his wife Angela, dog Zachary, and cats Bubz and Licorice.